Richard Strauss
An Owner's Manual

David Hurwitz

AMADEUS
PRESS

An Imprint of Hal Leonard Corporation

Published in 2014 by Amadeus Press
An Imprint of Hal Leonard Corporation
7777 West Bluemound Road
Milwaukee, WI 53213

Trade Book Division Editorial Offices
33 Plymouth St., Montclair, NJ 07042

Printed in the United States of America

Book design by Snow Creative Services

Library of Congress Cataloging-in-Publication Data

Hurwitz, David, 1961– author.
    Richard Strauss : an owner's manual / David Hurwitz.
      pages cm. — (Unlocking the masters series ; No. 25)
    ISBN 978-1-57467-442-2
1. Strauss, Richard, 1864–1949—Criticism and interpretation. I. Title.
    ML410.S93H87 2014
    780.92—dc23
                                                                    2014010594

www.amadeuspress.com

To Jim Bucar

Contents

Preface

Richard Strauss wrote a huge amount of music in every one of the major media of his day: symphonies, symphonic poems, choral works, operas, songs, piano solo, and chamber music. However, his reputation stands on the symphonic poems and operas of his maturity, and on his orchestral music more generally. For that reason, this survey will consider all of the major works with orchestra and many of the minor ones, including the operas and the orchestral songs. The songs with piano (approximately two hundred of them), chamber music, and choral works belong in a special category of their own (the songs), or are mostly early and/or atypical (the chamber music), or, in the case of the choral works, don't tell us anything especially significant that can't be found in Strauss's other vocal works.

There are also some major works that are barely known, or so seldom recorded that to spend time on them here when you can't purchase them to enjoy at home would be an exercise in frustration. So they will not be discussed, however much I might have liked to deal with them. As it is, I feel guilty—well, almost guilty—sending you off to find a piece with an unpronounceable name (even in German), such as *Panathenäenzug* for piano left-hand and orchestra, no matter how delightful and sadly neglected it is.

In this "owner's manual," as in others in this series, I have focused on strategies for listening. Strauss' music is "easy" in the sense that almost all of it is programmatic. That is, it describes an extramusical subject, and if you know the story behind the work, then you know the work, at least on one level, and nothing more need be said about it. For me, though, much of the fascination with Strauss' orchestral music resides in how he shapes and assembles his material into satisfying wholes whether you know anything about the program or not. I hope that this guide will suggest helpful ways to approach the music at this deeper level.

Strauss' operas and songs represent his lifelong attempt to find new, fresh, but always appropriate ways to tackle the issue of the relationship between text and music. Many of these works are little known, but all of them have something valuable to offer the listener, and it will be a very great pleasure to describe them to you. Operas and songs are even simpler to hear than programmatic symphonic music: you just follow the text or synopsis and enjoy the show. The only serious issue you might have is making sufficient time to get to know the music really well. That is a problem that no book can solve completely, but it can at least point your attention in the right direction so that the time you do have to invest will be spent productively.

In most of my guides for this series, including this one, I have taken great care to provide full orchestration lists for all of the works described. This was a major project, as most of Strauss' mature works employ very large orchestras with a notably complicated layout, and the actual scores are sometimes imprecise in giving complete lists of their instrumental requirements. The woodwind section, especially, contains a huge number of "doubling" parts—that is, a single musician plays multiple instruments. A flutist also plays the piccolo; the second oboe doubles on English horn, and the clarinets may take any member of that family. Strauss routinely calls for clarinets in A, B-flat, D, C, and E-flat, and bass clarinets in A and B-flat, plus basset horns, and so as not make things even more complicated, I have simplified the lists somewhat by sticking to raw numbers within each instrumental family—clarinets, for example—where the question is simply one of key rather than significant differences in range or timbre.

Aside from the fact that this is a book primarily about orchestral music, you actually can learn a great deal about a work before you even hear it simply by looking at its scoring. In particular, the relative numbers of woodwinds and strings quite often give a very strong indication of how the music is going to sound, whether the work (if it is an opera) will be comic or tragic, and what the composer's compositional strategy might have been. Does the lack of a part for contrabassoon signal a general lightness of texture? Does the huge brass section in

An Alpine Symphony anticipate the grandeur of the symphonic journey up the mountain before it even begins? Take a guess and see if your preconception turns out to be correct. Either way, it's a useful strategy to focus your attention when listening.

As with all the books in this series, there is no reason that you need to go through it in order. You can dip in at your pleasure, though I would suggest reading the introduction first, since it sets the stage and puts Strauss in a helpful context. Other than that, you should feel free to follow your own interests wherever they lead.

Acknowledgments

The author wishes to acknowledge very gratefully the help and support of everyone who contributed to the successful completion of this project, first and foremost series editor Bob Levine, as well as the team at Amadeus Press—John Cerullo, Jessica Burr, and copyeditor Angela Arcese (copyeditors never get the credit that they deserve, and it's an especially tough job in books like this, with titles in multiple languages, orchestration lists, and numerous formatting details). I also must thank Steve Miller, a dear friend and a serious Strauss aficionado, for sticking to his guns during a time when I doubted the value of much of Strauss' work. He was right all along. Lastly, many thanks to Strauss' publisher Boosey & Hawkes for making available scores of some difficult-to-find works, in particular his early Gluck arrangement *Iphigenie auf Tauris*. We badly need a decent recording.

Richard Strauss

Introduction
A First-Class Second-Rate Composer?

I n order to get a sense of the complexity and enduring fascination of Richard Strauss, both as a person and a musician, it is only necessary to consider the place and date of his birth, Munich in 1864, and that of his death, Garmisch (outside Munich) in 1949. In 1864, Munich was located in the independent kingdom of Bavaria. Germany did not exist as a political unity, and would not until 1871. The American Civil War was in full swing; Abraham Lincoln would be assassinated in the following year. By the time Strauss died in 1949, civilization as he knew it had been destroyed by two world wars, and recovery was just beginning. When he was born, the railroad was the latest innovation in transportation; shortly before his death, he was able to fly to England for a festival of his works.

In the world of music—German music specifically—by 1864 Wagner and Brahms were in midcareer. Liszt had just invented the symphonic poem. Strauss' father, Franz, was the principal horn player at the Bavarian Court Opera. By 1949, with European culture in as much of a shambles as Europe itself, the atonal revolution had swept through contemporary music. Schoenberg's theory of twelve-tone composition vied with the neoclassicism of composers such as Stravinsky and Hindemith. American jazz was all the rage, and "serious" classical music was quickly losing its centrality in the cultural life of the middle classes. Music making moved out of the home and, thanks to radio and recording technology, became the province of professionals, bolstered by large public and private corporations. Strauss spent much of his career in service to aristocrats, and ended it self-employed.

Set against the massive upheavals that occurred around him, Strauss' personal life could hardly have been less controversial. He was happily and faithfully married to a singer, Pauline de Ahna, who was born a year before him and died a year after. He adored her, and she him. Their relationship was stimulating, enduring, and wholly productive despite (or because of) their very different characters. They had one son, Franz, who together with his wife Alice went into the "family business"—they became Strauss' managers. His wife, son, daughter-in-law, and their two children were the most important things in Strauss' life, alongside his music. Indeed, the two often intermingled.

Strauss saw no reason why his comfortably middle-class home life was not a legitimate source of musical inspiration, most obviously in works such as the tone poem *Symphonia Domestica* and the opera *Intermezzo*. He worked tirelessly to professionalize the status of composers, fighting ceaselessly to improve copyright law and better organize the administration of German musical life. Despite his personal success, he suffered near financial ruin twice, after each world war. His concern with the mundane aspects of his profession earned him a reputation for being shallow and mercenary, part of a "bad boy" aspect of his personality that he actively cultivated and actually seemed at times to relish.

Strauss handled those in authority with a characteristically nineteenth-century combination of public servility mixed with private contempt, a formula that worked well for him until his unfortunate dealings with the Nazis. Against the fact that he used his status as Germany's greatest living composer to save his Jewish daughter-in-law and two grandsons from almost certain death, we must contrast the fact that he was pleased, at least for a brief time, to try to exploit the power of Hitler's regime to his own advantage. That he completely misjudged his situation can best be summarized by the image of him driving up to the gate of the Terezin concentration camp and demanding to see his daughter-in-law's relatives, who were imprisoned there (later to perish in the Holocaust). The guards thought he was a nut and sent him away.

Strauss' life story has been well told in a number of recent biographies, and because this is a book about his music, we shall only touch on those aspects of immediate concern to the works under discussion. He wrote a great deal of music—about three hundred individual compositions in all—and the more popular titles remain just the tip of the Straussian iceberg. With a few noteworthy exceptions at either end, such as the early First Horn Concerto and the late *Four Last Songs*, the music on which his reputation rests was composed roughly between 1890 and 1920. This period encompasses his artistic maturity through middle age. Yet there is so much more than that, and knowledge of his broader output yields an incomparably richer and, for the listener, more enjoyable experience.

It is certainly fair to say that Strauss was born with a musical silver spoon in his mouth. The son of one of the most highly respected musicians in Germany, he had every opportunity to acquire a first-class musical education and interact with the most noteworthy figures in German musical life. The conductor of the Court Opera in Munich, Hans von Bülow, for example, would eventually become his mentor. Bülow (1830–1894) was without question one of the greatest musical figures of the age. And although Richard's father, Franz, detested modern music, he still played first horn in the world premieres of several Wagner operas and other new works, all of which the younger Strauss had the opportunity to witness and absorb.

Today we value Richard Strauss solely as a composer, but during his lifetime he was equally in demand as a conductor, holding major posts in Meiningen, Munich, Berlin, and Vienna, among other places. He also played violin (in the semiprofessional orchestra his dad conducted in his spare time) and piano, gradually giving up both, save for recital tours with his wife. It was Strauss' musical skill on the podium, combined with his notorious reputation as an avant-garde composer, that led to his exceptional success from about 1890 onward. His musical career was not entirely smooth sailing, but it was about as ideally prepared as it possibly could have been. He still had to compete for recognition, but he seldom had to fight.

Perhaps the single greatest determining factor in Strauss' trajectory as a composer was the fact that he was ethnically German. This may seem an obvious point, but in the late nineteenth century this had very specific and significant musical implications, not just for his performing career, but also for the kind of composer that he ultimately became. Specifically, if you consider some of the other composers in this series of guides, who were contemporaries of Strauss and who also worked within the German tradition—Dvořák, Mahler, and Sibelius—you will find that they were all symphonists. Strauss was not, even though he called a couple of symphonic poems "symphonies" and wrote two early works in the genre. The reason for this distinction offers a useful way of placing Strauss in musical history.

By the end of the nineteenth century, the German symphony was as good as dead. This does not mean that composers stopped writing symphonies—far from it. But the fact is that there are no German symphonists after Brahms and Bruckner, both gone by the mid-1890s, whose music we care about today. Not one. Let me clarify this point a bit with reference to two twentieth-century German composers. Kurt Weill, for example, wrote two fine symphonies, but he is best known for this theater works, such as *The Threepenny Opera*. Paul Hindemith wrote symphonies, but just as often he cast his abstract orchestral pieces in unique, proprietary forms, as is the case with his *Konzertmusik* series. His popular *Symphonic Metamorphosis of Themes by Carl Maria von Weber* is a four-movement work completely symphonic in structure, but Hindemith denied it that title, while two of his symphonies, *Mathis der Maler* and *The Harmony of the World*, are suites arranged from operas.

In short, when later German composers, at least the really good ones, wrote orchestral music, they tended either to avoid focusing on symphonies completely, or to use the term *symphony* in a loose and generalized sort of way, much as Strauss himself did in writing a tone poem that he happened to call *An Alpine Symphony*. This tendency can be explained as the natural result of two simultaneous historical trends, one conservative, the other progressive.

Perhaps the most famous musical battle of the nineteenth century took place in Germany between the followers of Brahms and those of Wagner. The Brahms faction was considered to be conservative; the Wagnerians were the progressives, or avant-garde. Both sides claimed to be the legitimate heirs of the Viennese classical tradition of Haydn, Mozart, and Beethoven. Mozart, for example, was Strauss' favorite composer, an untouchable ideal, with Beethoven not too far behind. Haydn was highly respected in Strauss' youth, but more as the precursor of his two younger colleagues, while Bach was still in the process of being rediscovered.

The main difference between the two groups, though, was that Brahms worked in the traditional, abstract instrumental media: sonata, concerto, various chamber ensembles, and above all, the symphony. Wagner wrote operas almost exclusively. Brahms wrote nothing for the theater at all. The result of this bifurcation and specialization was that, with the exception of the "Wagnerian" symphonist Bruckner, whose music was highly controversial and unpopular until long after his death, symphonies were regarded as belonging squarely in the conservative camp. Legitimate, German symphonies by German composers thus had to be written according to tried-and-true rules of construction, even down to permissible orchestration.

It is difficult for listeners today to understand just how stifling these aesthetic standards were. Even in France, when composer César Franck wrote a symphony (his famous Symphony in D Minor) having only three movements and employing an English horn and a harp, a near riot occurred at its 1889 premiere among an audience of listeners with very fixed notions of what such works could be. Symphonies just didn't do that sort of thing. They were supposed to be models of compositional and aural sobriety—never mind that the classical composers would have been shocked at the very idea. Strauss' early symphonies follow this conservative pattern; they are strikingly well made and, true to their textbook origins, strikingly unoriginal.

Dvořák, Mahler, and Sibelius all in their various ways wrote symphonies that advanced the possibilities of the genre, but all three were "outsiders," ethnically or culturally. Dvořák was Czech, Sibelius Finnish. Both had a local base of operations and an open field within which they could find ways to give the German symphony a flavor regarded as simultaneously individual and nationalistic. Mahler was both Czech and Jewish, a fact that encouraged him to synthesize a personal, eclectic symphonic language that aesthetically was wholly antithetical to the purist, German school. He was largely rejected as a composer during his lifetime, especially in Germany, for both musical and racial reasons.

Strauss admired Mahler and actively promoted his music but never challenged him as a symphonist. This may have been because Strauss was the ultimate "insider." His evolution as a composer, from conservative to radical, took place entirely within the conventions of the German tradition in which he was raised. Even at his most radical, Strauss never had his right of participation in that tradition questioned, and he in turn took its assumptions, including that of its inherent superiority to all other national schools, completely for granted. Under the watchful eye of his resolutely reactionary father, he grew up to revere the Viennese classics as the pinnacle of musical achievement. As for those who came later, Mendelssohn was cautiously admired. Schumann, whose Fourth Symphony remains one of the most formally adventurous of the early romantic period, was seen as selectively interesting but potentially dangerous.

Among living composers, some kind words were reserved for the classically inclined Germanophile Frenchman Camille Saint-Saëns. So when Strauss self-deprecatingly referred to himself as "a first-class second-rate composer," it pays to keep in mind just who he thought the first-rate composers were: Mozart, Beethoven, and ultimately, Wagner. If Strauss hesitated to place himself on their level, he certainly had no issue positioning himself at or near the top of the heap containing everyone else. Always frank about his strengths and weaknesses, he would have been the last to claim that everything he wrote was equally worthy, but also the first to insist that it was better than what anyone else at the time was doing. He was, in short, every inch the self-absorbed, romantic artist.

Strauss' first step "outside of the box" as a composer, then, was understandably in the direction of Brahms, Germany's modern conservative. This may have been motivated by the heavy involvement in Brahms of his mentor in Meiningen, Hans von Bülow, and consequently Strauss' own acquaintance with the composer, whose music he conducted. Strauss' "Brahms period" lasted only a few years in the mid-1880s. It was not long before he was comparing the German composer unflatteringly to the quirky Frenchman Hector Berlioz. Significantly, Strauss' most Brahmsian composition is the 1886 *Burleske* for piano and orchestra—in other words, a parody. Strauss was a great musical humorist, but as so often is the case in the very serious world of classical music, not everyone got the joke. Bülow, for whom the work was written, hated the *Burleske* and never played it (though he did conduct it).

With Brahms out of the way as a compositional model, Strauss turned, perhaps inevitably, to Wagner; or more correctly, Liszt/Wagner. Brahms had a following, but the Wagnerites represented a full-blown cult. Their high priestess was the composer's fanatically devoted but not necessarily musical widow Cosima, Liszt's daughter and Bülow's first wife. She and her crew were quite simply a bunch of loons, convinced of the transfiguring power of Wagner's music when placed in the service of a toxic concoction of racist German nationalism, Schopenhauerian philosophy, and Christian mysticism. Strauss was on good terms with Cosima during the 1890s, until it became clear that he was developing his own musical personality and an orchestral technique that in some ways outstripped Wagner's own. This was of course intolerable, for cults demand obedient followers, not original creative geniuses.

Suffice it say that Strauss was one of the very few *echt*-German composers of the day who was able to separate his admiration of Wagner the composer from adherence to the Wagner cult, taking what he needed to bring German opera and orchestral music triumphantly into the twentieth century. Just how he did it will form a large part of the discussion of the individual works that follows. In the meantime, it will be profitable to consider what the Liszt/Wagner school meant to a modern composer of orchestral music in the late nineteenth century from a purely technical point of view, because this will provide the key to understanding the project that occupied Strauss throughout his mature creative life.

Consider the two lists that follow, setting forth the instrumentation of Strauss' Symphony No. 2 of 1884, and then the tone poem *Till Eulenspiegel's Merry Pranks* of a decade later (1895 to be exact):

Symphony No. 2 in F Minor

2 flutes, 2 oboes, 2 clarinets, 2 bassoons, 4 horns, 2 trumpets, 3 trombones, tuba, 1 pair of timpani, strings

Till Eulenspiegel's Merry Pranks

piccolo, 3 flutes, 3 oboes, English horn, 3 clarinets, bass clarinet, 3 bassoons, contrabassoon, 8 horns, 6 trumpets, 3 trombones, tuba, 4 timpani, bass drum, snare drum, cymbals, triangle, large ratchet (cog rattle), strings

You don't need to know anything about music in general to see immediately that the scoring of the tone poem is much fuller than that of the symphony. In fact, Strauss' Second Symphony, with the exception of the tuba, uses the standard romantic symphonic ensemble of the mid-to-late nineteenth century, the same forces we find in the symphonies of Schumann and Brahms. Now, there could be room for an extra instrument or two—a contrabassoon here, a piccolo or perhaps a triangle there—but in the main, this was the basic setup. Strauss' First Symphony uses this same orchestra, minus the tuba. There was a good practical reason for preferring this layout: it was what most small towns and aristocratic courts could afford, and if you wanted your music to get played, these were the constraints.

Accordingly, Strauss' symphony achieved an impressive number of performances in the years immediately following its composition, and it became quite popular. It established him as a composer who could achieve attractive and enjoyable results working within the limitations of the German symphonic tradition. There is a paradox here. The reality under which German composers worked bore scant relationship to the theoretical significance of the German symphony as the highest, most sophisticated, most profound form of large-ensemble music. That was certainly true in the classical period; but a variety of factors—including the sheer proliferation of orchestras of mediocre quality and the need to cater to the demands of a growing, and largely conservative, middle-class public—conspired to stifle both the formal and sonic possibilities inherent in new symphonic music.

With few exceptions, then, the late romantic German symphony was a dumbed-down shadow of its former, classical self, a used Volkswagen being passed off as a new Mercedes. It was impossible that any composer of more than average ability would not have been aware of this fact, if only through the inevitable comparison of most modern works with their avowed models. This does not mean that there were no great German symphonic composers in the mid-to-late nineteenth century. We know that there were, but you can count them on the fingers of one hand: Mendelssohn, Schumann, Brahms, and Bruckner, basically. The rest, names such as Raff, Bruch, Spohr, Reinecke, Draeseke, and countless others—some very popular for a while—have been relegated to the mediocre middle as the true "second raters." Wagner famously declared that the symphony was "dead." He was wrong, of course, for the world outside Germany, but for Wagner there was no world outside Germany, so he didn't care. Within Germany, he had a point.

The situation was rather different when it came to music for the theater. Here, for example, is the instrumentation of Wagner's revolutionary 1859 opera *Tristan und Isolde*, an ensemble that is not particularly large either for Wagner or for the period more generally:

Tristan und Isolde
> piccolo, 3 flutes, 2 oboes, English horn, 2 clarinets, bass clarinet, 3 bassoons, 4 horns, 2 trumpets, 3 trombones, tuba, timpani, triangle, cymbals, harp, strings (plus 6 horns, 3 trumpets, and 3 trombones offstage)

As you can plainly see, this is much closer to the scoring of *Till Eulenspiegel* than it is to Strauss' Second Symphony. What Strauss has done, and what composers such as Mahler did also, is to take the full range of coloristic possibilities available to composers of opera and other forms of theatrical music, and use them in works intended for the concert hall. They were not the first to do this; there has always been a certain amount of crosstalk between symphonic and theatrical music, and Strauss had a direct and remarkable precedent in the works of Hector Berlioz, who preceded everyone else in this regard. But Berlioz was French, and his symphonies (*Symphonie fantastique, Harold in Italy, Romeo and Juliet*) were hybrid works whose pictorial and programmatic elements placed them well outside the conventions of the German symphonic tradition, Beethoven's "Pastoral" Symphony notwithstanding.

Once again, it can be difficult for modern listeners to understand what all the fuss was about regarding a seemingly trivial matter such as the actual choice of instruments, but it is important to understand that for audiences in previous centuries, certain instrumental timbres had very specific pictorial connotations. The English horn, for example, was associated with pastoral music, shepherd's pipes, and rural scenes. Bass drum, cymbals, and triangle were "Turkish" instruments of war, quite literally, and represented both military episodes and exotic, oriental subjects. Harps were used for love music, or touching farewells—including death, with its attendant thoughts of heaven. These and other unusual sounds risked distracting the listener's attention from the abstract, pure, and therefore loftier emotions allegedly the exclusive province of the symphony, instead conjuring up concrete images of mundane objects: battles, herds of sheep and cows, birds, storms, or (God forbid) sex.

The decision to exploit the full resources of modern theatrical scoring along the lines of Wagner and Berlioz thus meant that as a German composer Strauss had to abandon his efforts to write symphonies. Unlike Mahler, who consciously attempted to redefine the parameters of what "symphony" meant, Strauss accepted the conventional German view, not just for artistic reasons, but also as a shrewd career move. He understood, as the more idealistic Mahler did not, that he could get away with all kinds of formal, harmonic, and instrumental audacities in the name of storytelling—for all three go hand in hand—that would have been rejected vehemently in the field of symphonic composition. So he began writing symphonic poems (Strauss called them "tone poems") after the example of Liszt, who is credited with inventing, or at least systematizing, the form.

Liszt's concept for the symphonic poem involved taking one basic musical idea, or theme, and transforming it into a number of related motives and melodies according to the programmatic concept, or story, that he was attempting to illustrate. He accomplished this goal with widely varying success. Strauss, as you will hear, was both more subtle and varied in his approach, as well as more consistently successful. Part of the reason was Strauss' tremendous skill as an orchestrator. This talent is a gift. For example, Berlioz had it, but his best friend Liszt, for all of his interesting ideas and colorful presentation, did not. The ability to make a beautiful or simply intriguing noise is incredibly valuable, particularly if the musical themes themselves are not especially distinctive, or the programmatic concept requires the imaginative use of sound without the crutch of an actual tune.

In his tone poems, Strauss pushed the concept of descriptive music to entirely new heights, and so became the leader of the modern German school. Each tone poem premiere was a major event, avidly reported on and discussed in the press both in Germany and throughout the musical world. The ability to play one of his large, complex, and virtuosic pieces became a source of pride among the world's great orchestras. Strauss was not writing for the provinces. Although his subject matter might be popular, funny, autobiographical, or pseudo-epic, the musical apparatus he employed and the technical standards he required were consistently on the very highest level. Contemporary critics noticed this and did not fail to accuse him of lavishing extravagant resources on trivial or controversial subjects, but that only served to heighten his notoriety and broaden his appeal. There is no such thing as bad publicity.

The tone poems of the late 1880s and 1890s were in any case little more than a huge and glittering preparation for Strauss' true calling: opera. Finding the answer to the problem of how to write German opera after Wagner was bound to be a difficult task, and Strauss approached it with a typical mixture of caution and audacity: caution, because he took his time after the failure of his first opera, *Guntram*, in 1894 to steer clear of the medium until he felt able to approach it on his own terms; audacity, because once he found his path, he leapt forward with breathtaking sureness and scored one huge success after another in a remarkably short period of time: *Salome* in 1905, *Elektra* in 1909, and *Der Rosenkavalier* in 1911.

These three works immediately entered the repertoire of opera houses the world over, an astonishing feat, especially if you know any-thing about the issues of cost, ego, and sheer insanity that dominate the world of operatic production. They cemented Strauss' reputation as Germany's, and arguably the world's, greatest living composer. The operas and tone poems also helped to establish the careers of many of the world's major conductors, for Strauss understood that it was better for him to have his music performed by others than by himself, how-ever much he might be in demand for that purpose. In fact, he always said that conducting his own music bored him, and indeed the many recordings of it that he left behind, while never less than profession- ally adequate, seldom rise to the level achieved by the best of his later interpreters: noted names such as Fritz Reiner, George Szell, Rudolf Kempe, Karl Böhm, Herbert von Karajan, Herbert Blomstedt, and numerous others.

From the 1920s on, Strauss had to endure the indignity of having outlived his reputation as a composer in the vanguard of musical progress. Perhaps that was inevitable. It happened to many long-lived composers in the twentieth century, especially those who were self- conscious about maintaining their modernity. Radicalism always comes with a built-in expiration date. Stravinsky spent the last two decades of his life playing a musical game of "catch-up," and so, to a lesser extent, did Aaron Copland.

Having arrived at a style that suited him, Strauss felt no obligation to follow his colleagues into what has turned out to be in retrospect—at least for the most part—the dead end of atonal or serial (twelve-tone) composition. This took a certain degree of artistic courage, and the fact that Strauss abandoned the notion of musical "progress" as a function of ever-increasing dissonance and the technical rules for controlling it does not mean that he stopped refining and reinventing his art. Rather than denigrating late Strauss as nostalgic and regressive, it makes more sense to try to understand what his concerns were as an opera composer, and how he addressed them.

First and foremost, Strauss wanted to write comedies, which makes him unique among twentieth-century writers of opera, never mind German ones. His goal, he claimed, was to become "the Offenbach of the twentieth century." To anyone who knows and loves *Salome* and *Elektra*, this may come as a shock. However, comedy in opera does not necessarily mean laugh-out-loud hilarity, but rather wit, amusing repartee, and above all an exploration of the foibles and frailties of the relationships between normal people muddling through life. It doesn't matter if these people are real or mythical, and Strauss believed that a marital spat was as fit a subject for the stage as any grand historical tragedy.

Strauss was not interested in the usual "boy meets girl and one or both die horribly" operatic plot. Few composers had a greater gift for expressing love in music, whether cerebral, erotic, depraved, or merely graphically sexual. He knew that he had a genuine talent in this direction, and if it was good enough for Mozart, then it was just fine for Strauss too. He had a legitimate personal conception of opera that only recently has begun to be taken seriously, thanks in large part to the leveling effect of passing time. We no longer care that his music may have been starting to sound out of date in 1935 compared to what the younger generation was doing. Their works sound out of date now too, some of them much more so than Strauss ever will.

Today, when the musical battle of tonal versus atonal music is largely as dead an issue as the nineteenth-century Brahms–Wagner controversy, Strauss' late works are being revived and reappraised. Their consummate technique, ravishing orchestration, and melodic beauty have always been self-evident, but it is becoming clearer that Strauss' dogged pursuit of his own individual path was not the result of mere petulance or antagonism to modern trends after the World War I, but rather a genuine, evolving exploration of the relationship between words and music in the service of an aesthetic unique in its emphasis on the value and necessity of loving and compassionate human relationships.

Strauss may have been happiest when he felt he was pushing his musical boundaries, whether this was duly recognized or not; but throughout his career he also wrote plenty of good music within traditional forms, including concertos, ballets, suites, and above all, a huge and highly varied collection of songs, some forty of which were orchestrated. When a composer writes a large number of indisputable masterpieces on the grandest scale, it's very easy to ignore or disparage the less ambitious works. This would be a mistake. They are no less "Straussian" than their larger cousins, and no picture of his achievement is complete without giving them due consideration. More to the point, they are very enjoyable and worth getting to know.

From a purely biographical point of view, Strauss will always be an enigmatic figure. Even making allowances for the inherent mystery of musical genius, it just isn't possible to wrap our brains around a man whose life and creativity encompassed the period from the unification of Germany in 1871 to the defeat of Hitler in 1945. The upheavals in society, politics, and art are simply too convulsive, and the constantly shifting historical grounds limit our ability to find the most useful context in which to reconcile Strauss' public and private personas. But if the man remains a puzzle that admits of no solution, the same is certainly not true of his music, a fact that the following pages hopefully will demonstrate.

Part 1

Orchestral Music Without Voices

Symphonies, Concertos, and Serenades

S trauss' reputation may rest on his operas and tone poems, but as noted in the Introduction, he composed a great quantity of music in traditional forms, and he did it throughout his career. In addition, he also left a large amount of occasional music—fanfares, preludes, and festival pieces—that do not need to be discussed here and which you often will find as fillers to many recordings of the more popular works. What you need to keep in mind when considering the symphonies, concertos, and works for wind ensemble is that the style of the music is often determined by the purpose for which is was composed.

Concertos, in particular, tend to be more traditional in form and content, because they would have to be if they stood any chance of being championed by major soloists. This is as true of modern music today as it was in Strauss' time. A concerto, if not written for a specific artist, is still a collaboration between the composer and that imaginary, great virtuoso whose cooperation is essential to breathe life into the work. Strauss took care to make sure that his concertos, difficult and brilliant as they are, invariably reward the soloist who plays them. All of them are considered here, save for a couple of brief, early concertante works, the Romances for Clarinet and Cello, respectively, which you can explore at your leisure.

The music for wind ensembles is Strauss' most affectionate tribute to Mozart, and it is all extremely charming. All of the major classical composers wrote wind serenades for the ensembles kept by their aristocratic patrons, but only Mozart regularly wrote great music for the medium, most notably the massive and glorious "Gran Partita," K. 361 (also known as his Serenade No. 10) for thirteen winds, the largest work of its kind, and Strauss' basic model. After the classical period, the idiom virtually died out, except in the Czech lands, where it popped up one last gorgeous time in the form of Dvořák's Wind Serenade. Strauss was the only great composer subsequently to write a series of important works for a large mixed group of woodwind instruments (with horns). They are staples of the wind ensemble repertoire but still far less well known to most collectors than they deserve to be.

Here, then, is a brief survey of a side of Strauss that many listeners do not know and, with the exception of such popular pieces as the First Horn Concerto or the very late Oboe Concerto, may not have heard. All of this music has been recorded, often more than once, and should not prove too difficult to find for those interested. These pieces reveal Strauss' great versatility and range, and also his delight is solving compositional problems of a kind quite different from those he set himself in the operas and tone poems.

The Two Symphonies

Some commentators have remarked very cleverly that Strauss' two symphonies are not terribly original. The fact is, they weren't meant to be. Consider that when Strauss wrote his Second Symphony, Brahms' Third, Tchaikovsky's Fourth, Bruckner's Seventh, and Dvořák's Sixth had all been composed, and all are far more "modern" than Strauss' two efforts in the form. Strauss intentionally designed them as musical calling cards evidencing his right of participation in the great German symphonic tradition in which he was raised, and this they certainly achieved. Viewed from this perspective, and if we suppress the urge to play that tired old game of "let's find evidence of the mature composer to come," they are attractive and enjoyable works all by themselves.

Symphony No. I (1880)
Scoring: 2 flutes, 2 oboes, 2 clarinets, 2 bassoons, 4 horns, 2 trumpets, 3 trombones, timpani, strings

Strauss was only sixteen years old when he composed his First Symphony. He was proud of it at the time, and, more to the point, so was his father. It was well received at its initial performances but soon fell into oblivion in the face of the much more accomplished Second Symphony. Strauss actually encouraged its suppression, having no illusions about its absolute quality. For the work of a sixteen-year-old fledgling composer, it's not a bad piece, but it is no work of genius either. It was not Strauss' first orchestral work; he had been composing overtures, marches, dances, and the like for some years, and his handling of the traditional orchestra here is remarkably assured.

Specifically, this roughly thirty-five-minute work in the usual four movements reveals that Strauss has learned the most important major lesson in writing orchestral music: that great orchestration depends on the handling of the woodwind section. There are many reasons why this should be the case. The woodwind section, which really includes the French horns as well, is the most timbrally varied of all, but the limited numbers of each instrument force the composer to use them either as solos or in a multitude of colorful combinations—at least, that's the theory.

The presence of a single "specialty" member of the family—a piccolo, an English horn, a contrabassoon, or a bass clarinet—can change the entire sound of the work. Mozart's music gained a wholly unique sensuous smoothness from the use of clarinets. The piccolo part in Brahms' Second Serenade completely changes the complexion of music scored mostly for "low" instruments (it has no violins). Strauss' use of his woodwinds, both alone and in groups, especially in the central section of the third-movement Scherzo (called a "trio") of the First Symphony, shows that he had already grasped the right ideas.

Finally, good orchestration covers any number of compositional weaknesses, just as a great tune tends to make all other considerations nearly irrelevant. Strauss was not the most distinctive of tunesmiths, but a great composer doesn't have to be. Wagner wasn't, either; neither was, say, Shostakovich, or Bruckner. Brahms, who constantly extolled the value of a good tune, always remained slightly jealous of Dvořák. Just as important in the grand scheme of things is knowing how to present your material and what to do with it, and there Strauss was a master from the beginning. Colorful scoring that captivates the ear and never fatigues or bores the listener makes a work sound shorter than it really is, even one that has a rather stiff little fugue in the middle of its finale, as does the First Symphony.

Symphony No. 2 (1883–84)
Scoring: 2 flutes, 2 oboes, 2 clarinets, 2 bassoons, 4 horns, 2 trumpets, 3 trombones, tuba, timpani, strings

By the time of the Second Symphony, only four years later, Strauss had developed very audibly into a much more confident composer. The handling of the brass, in particular, is much freer and more colorful. He was beginning to understand the possibilities of each instrument and was worrying less about whether or not that potential could be exploited within the German symphonic tradition. Still, he was willing to push it only so far. We need to keep in mind that Berlioz's phantasmagoric *Symphonie fantastique* was already half a century old, and Mahler's First was just on the horizon, but that does not lessen Strauss' achievement taken on its own.

Formally, the work is also more interesting than its predecessor. Strauss places the Scherzo second, as Beethoven did in his Ninth Symphony (and Bruckner would do shortly in his Eighth). Clearly, he was giving more thought to matters of balance and large-scale form. Although about five minutes longer than the First Symphony, the music seems to move more freely, and that's the sort of writing that cheats the clock from the listener's perspective. The more colorful scoring also encourages Strauss to create themes that suit the individual instruments that play them (initially) to a greater degree, and in the finale, music from the previous movements returns toward the end.

This use of cyclical form, as it's called, may also be a nod to the Beethoven of the Ninth Symphony, though contemporary audiences would have perceived it as a modern touch. Brahms, who regarded the work somewhat condescendingly as "very pretty," seemed not to approve of Strauss' use of thematic recall in the finale, never mind that fact that he made extensive use of the same technique in his just-completed Third Symphony, possibly taking a hint from Dvořák's earlier Fifth Symphony. You often never know where or how these things get started.

The Second Symphony received its premiere in New York, of all places, with Theodore Thomas leading the New York Philharmonic in December 1884. It was very successful. Thomas was a friend of Strauss' father, Franz, and got his hands on the manuscript during a trip to Germany. Thomas would prove a loyal supporter of Strauss, especially after his move to Chicago in 1891, so that orchestra's glorious Strauss tradition dates back well over a century. I mention this detail because it reveals, first, the growing internationalization of the musical world toward the end of the nineteenth century, but more importantly because it reminds us that Strauss' later works required the existence of a large, permanent, orchestral infrastructure in order for them to be possible at all.

Critics often remark that these symphonies remain only partially successful from a formal point of view, and that may well be true. You may notice development sections that develop either too much or not enough, and the occasional moment where the music loses its sense of direction or seems to run on longer than might be strictly ideal. However, this only matters, really, if the result is boring. One talent Strauss had from the very outset was a certain easy fluency, "the gift of gab," as the great writer on music Donald Francis Tovey put it (referring to Handel). Detractors cite this quality as evidence of his music's tendency toward empty note spinning, but I see it more charitably. If you aren't going to be profound, then at least be entertaining. Strauss is nearly always that.

Concertos for Violin, Horn, Piano, and Oboe, and a Woodwind Duet

Violin Concerto (1882)
Scoring: 2 flutes, 2 oboes, 2 clarinets, 2 bassoons, 4 horns, 2 trumpets, timpani, violin solo, strings

Many listeners find themselves surprised at the very existence of a violin concerto by Strauss, never mind the fact that it's his first work in the form. Strauss was apparently a very decent violinist—he played in his father's amateur orchestra—but the concerto was composed for his teacher Benno Walter, who was concertmaster of the Munich Court Orchestra and also Franz Strauss' first cousin. It is a telling indication of the difference between the "concerto tradition" and the latest trends in orchestral music more generally that Strauss was still conducting the work in the 1890s, long past the point where his own idiom had evolved beyond recognition. It must have seemed hopelessly old-fashioned to him, but the rules governing concerto writing were, if anything, even more rigid than those governing the symphony, and the work had its proponents. So who was he to argue?

Violin concertos are atrociously difficult to write. They require an intimate knowledge of the instrument's technique, plus a keen feeling for orchestral balance and color, leaving aside the always-tricky matters of formal construction more generally. Then there are the violinists themselves, much crankier as a group than pianists and other soloists for reasons that are difficult to pinpoint. In a very real sense, the violin literature is a world unto itself, and unlike pianists, who spend much of their time as humble accompanists, violinists are always soloists, with egos to match. A pianist will begin life as a mere accompanist and gradually evolve into a concert artist worthy of solo billing, but a violinist always begins intent on a solo career, and the ones who wind up in the string section of an orchestra have already failed on the highest level. So they tend to be, let us say, just a bit touchy.

Violinists generally also have much shorter careers than pianists. Like singers, their prime lasts as long as their left hands remain supple and their bow arms responsive, and this varies widely with the individual. Since the technique for left and right hands is completely different and needs to be acquired independently, the violin is a much more difficult instrument to play well than the piano, and also much harder to write for. Brahms, who knew the instrument as well as anyone, still sought out the advice of Joseph Joachim in writing his Violin Concerto. Beethoven had help from his dedicatee, Franz Clement, as well. Joachim drove Dvořák, himself an immensely experienced string player, crazy over his Violin Concerto, and then never played the finished work. Most important romantic composers, for similar reasons, wrote only a single violin concerto, if they wrote one at all.

It is therefore all the more remarkable that Strauss composed one so early in his career and did it so well. There may be few audible signs of the composer to come, but there can be no stronger evidence that he had the talent to become *something*. His concerto is effectively constructed, full of good if not always distinctive tunes, and scored with unfailing accuracy and imagination. Yes, the work is derivative, especially in the tarantella finale, which marries the orchestral lightness of Mendelssohn's Violin Concerto to the finale of the "Italian" Symphony. Lasting almost exactly half an hour, Strauss' concerto is also just the right length to give the soloist a chance to strut his stuff before collapsing from exhaustion.

The Violin Concerto has been making a bit of a comeback in recent years thanks to recordings, and also the number of excellent soloists looking for repertoire by major composers than hasn't been played to death. It's an interesting question in musical aesthetics to wonder if the work would be much more popular had Strauss' later tone poems not been written. We have an instinctive and wholly reasonable tendency to base our expectations of any composer's work on his most famous pieces, and we reject as second rate anything that does not meet them. The Violin Concerto is certainly not bad as far as nineteenth-century violin concertos go, even if, for all of the evident talent that it reveals, it just doesn't sound much like Strauss.

Horn Concerto No. 1 (1882–83)
Scoring: 2 flutes, 2 oboes, 2 clarinets, 2 bassoons, 2 horns, 2 trumpets, timpani, solo horn, strings

Horn Concerto No. 2 (1942)
Scoring: 2 flutes, 2 oboes, 2 clarinets, 2 bassoons, 2 horns, 2 trumpets, timpani, solo horn, strings

Strauss' two horn concertos are the only two such works since Mozart's to have entered the international repertoire with any regularity. They date from opposite ends of his career but, as you can see, feature exactly the same scoring, and so really belong together as a pair. Stylistically, they reveal the difference between a classicizing style and the real thing. The first is an imitation, and a very good one, but by 1942, Strauss had arrived at his own personal idiom that was truly classical in its elegance, balanced proportions, and originality.

The First Concerto was composed for Strauss' father, Franz, but interestingly not dedicated to him—at least not in the version for horn and orchestra (as opposed to horn and piano for home use). Franz Strauss never played it in public. He considered its high notes too risky, and he was evidently a nervous player to begin with. Horn players are notoriously high-strung, the instrument being famously treacherous, and Franz Strauss played the valveless natural horn, or *Waldhorn*. Interestingly, Strauss' concerto, which Franz reportedly performed at home with his son at the piano, is not fully playable on the *Waldhorn*, so it's a bit of a mystery how he did it, or if he merely adapted the work as Strauss wrote it for his personal use.

Writing for the horn is a very specialized affair. Today, horn parts usually are composed for the standard instrument in the key of F, with the players transposing between keys as necessary depending on the instrument that they use. Strauss enjoyed retaining the old-fashioned notation with horn parts written in various keys as per the musical context, and he stuck with that method throughout his life. It was certainly a legacy he acquired from his father, who also wrote an attractive horn concerto of his own (it has been recorded).

The First Concerto is only fifteen minutes long and features a "hunting" finale very similar to those in Mozart's concertos. A high-spirited, muscular, bravura work, it gives the soloist the opportunity to do just about everything that the horn of the day could, but Strauss is careful to keep the piece brief. Concertos for any instruments that depend on human breath to create sound are extremely tiring for the player, and the timbre of the horn itself can be just as fatiguing for the listener. You might say the difference between a wind concerto and a string or keyboard concerto is similar, musically speaking, to the difference between a sprint and a marathon.

Strauss dedicated his Second Concerto to his father's memory. It lasts about twenty minutes, which is about as long as is technically feasible. In keeping with Strauss' late style, the music is somewhat lighter in texture, more nimble in rhythm, and harmonically more adventurous than in the First Concerto. Instead of a "hunting" finale, Strauss offers a scherzo that requires an almost superhuman amount of agility from the soloist. It also features a sort of "Cheer, Boys, Cheer" theme beginning with four repeated notes and continuing tipsily thereafter, and this brings the piece to its rowdy conclusion.

Strauss' horn concertos are important works not just because there are so few good horn concertos in the repertoire. They tend to be regarded as standing somewhat apart from the main thread of his development, and it does seem reasonable to conclude that they exist only because of his father. In that sense, they are special. However, even if this is true, they reveal quite plainly that the neoclassical element of his compositional makeup was present from the start. It was not something he acquired during the composition of *Ariadne* and *Le bourgeois gentilhomme*, or just a passing phase, but an integral part of his music language to be used at will.

Indeed, there is a strong argument to be made that the radical tone poems and operas of the 1890s and early 1900s are in fact atypical. Viewed whole, over the long arc of his career, the history of Strauss' compositional development represents the unification of the innate classical tendencies of his youth with the more modern language and technique he acquired subsequently, and on which he staked his reputation. From this perspective, the two horn concertos, which reach across the decades to unite sixty years of unceasing musical activity, constitute prima facie evidence.

Oboe Concerto (1945)
Scoring: 2 flutes, English horn, 2 clarinets, 2 bassoons, 2 horns, solo oboe, strings

Strauss had a special relationship with the oboe, a fact that is all the more curious when you consider that he's best known, in the woodwind world, for his exploitation of the clarinet family, and in particular for his revival of Mozart's beloved basset horns (members of the family pitched midway between the standard and bass clarinets). The reality, though, is that Strauss treated clarinets as the violas among the wind instruments: essential, numerous, but seldom exploited for important solos. We need only consider Strauss' handling of the oboe in the second love scene in *Don Juan*, Dulcinea's melody in *Don Quixote*, or introducing the theme of the baby in the *Symphonia Domestica*, to understand that in Strauss' woodwind section, the oboe leads.

When American oboist John de Lancie asked Strauss in 1945 if he had ever considered writing a concerto for the instrument, Strauss simply told him "No," and the matter was dropped. De Lancie met Strauss during his tour of duty in the U.S. Army, which took pains to declare Strauss and his home in Garmisch "off limits" so that he could live unmolested following the war's end. Strauss, for his part, wrote the concerto after all, making sure that de Lancie, who went on to become the legendary principal oboist with the Philadelphia Orchestra, was given the rights to the first American performance. This turned out to be impossible, as de Lancie had just joined the Philadelphia Orchestra (from Pittsburgh) as second oboist to his original teacher, who was understandably mortified that his pupil had inspired a new concerto from a great composer such as Strauss. In order to avoid bad feelings, de Lancie ceded the rights to his friend in the CBS Symphony Orchestra, Mitch Miller, of *Sing Along with Mitch* fame. De Lancie died in 2002 but, happily, lived to make a splendid modern recording of the concerto that he inspired.

The Oboe Concerto lasts about twenty-five minutes and is practically unplayable as composed. Strauss loved writing endless cantilenas for all the woodwind instruments (horns too), leaving it up the player to figure out how to phrase the music without breathing, or die trying. Most oboists cheat and modify the part accordingly, even when they have the ability to use rotary breathing techniques to keep up a constant supply of wind. The timbre of the oboe, also, tends to be quite fatiguing in large quantities, and so the concerto really does represent the ne plus ultra of the art of great oboe playing.

It is also the only oboe concerto since the classical period to become a repertory item. As with the horn concertos, great composers after Mozart seldom found good reason to write large concerted works for oboe. If you were going to write a wind concerto, then the logical choice was the clarinet, and while scads of composers wrote adorable smaller works for their virtuoso friends, full-scale concertos for the oboe remained vanishingly scarce until Strauss seized the bull by the horns and produced his.

Although written in the conventional three movements, the work follows its own constantly evolving, rhapsodic form. It's sort of a jollier take on the same process found in *Metamorphosen*, which is discussed with the other tone poems. Cleverly scored for chamber orchestra with only a single English horn and no orchestral oboes, the piece begins with a tiny squiggle in the strings, and the whole work grows from there. The soloist enters immediately and plays for the first few minutes without pausing for air, or so it should seem, and all three movements have long passages of similar breadth.

The slow movement follows the first without a break, but you can hear that opening squiggle continuing underneath the new themes as the music proceeds. As in the finale of the Second Horn Concerto, Strauss writes a type of scherzo in the form of a rondo, or so it's called, adding plenty of rhythmic hijinks to the already fearsomely difficult solo line. Getting through it unscathed is just barely possible. Getting through it with beautiful tone, shapely phrasing, and careful attention to dynamics really is an astonishing feat and requires artistry of the highest sort—a classic musical instance, in de Lancie's case, of being careful what you wish for.

Duett-Concertino for Clarinet and Bassoon (1947)
Scoring: solo clarinet, solo bassoon, harp, strings

When Strauss finally did consider writing for solo clarinet, please note that he took care to invite a bassoon and a harp to the party. In addition, the strings are divided into a solo quintet versus the full section. The result, belying the simple-looking scoring, permits a huge variety of tone and texture, with the harp used very discreetly and with great sensitivity. I had the opportunity to hear this piece live while working on this book, and I can attest to the magical world that Strauss conjures up in this, his last purely orchestral work.

There's allegedly a programmatic story behind this piece: "Beauty and the Beast," or something along those lines. It's an entirely plausible theory, and I leave it to you to figure out which instrument is which. The work plays in three connected movements and unfolds as a series of duets almost operatic in nature. In the first movement, the clarinet leads with a long solo, while the bassoon gradually joins with gruff commentary. The slow movement, only a bit longer than three minutes, features the doleful bassoon with the clarinet answering, while the final rondo, the longest movement, is a playful series of episodes in which the two sing happily together.

As with the other wind concertos, the score is full of long, cantabile lines that run the risk of asphyxiating the players. Making matters even more fun, the two soloists often echo each other's melodies, or play in rhythmic unison, which makes cheating a lot harder than it would be if there were only a single solo line. Works such as this are unique; they have no true antecedents in the orchestral literature, and you are most likely to hear them on recordings or at those few concerts where the principal orchestral woodwinds get a rare solo opportunity. That Strauss wrote these final pieces at all is something miraculous.

Burleske for Piano and Orchestra (1885–86)
Scoring: piccolo, 2 flutes, 2 oboes, 2 clarinets, 2 bassoons, 4 horns, 2 trumpets, timpani, solo piano, strings

Strauss called none of his three works for piano and orchestra "concertos," but that is what they are, effectively, and contemporaries called them that at various times. The *Burleske* maintains a toehold in the repertoire and has been championed by some very major names, including Martha Argerich, Claudio Arrau, Rudolf Serkin, Glenn Gould, Sviatoslav Richter, and Nelson Freire. Strauss initially had doubts about it. These misgivings were encouraged by his mentor Hans von Bülow—who loathed the *Burleske* on account of its extreme difficulty—but Strauss came to enjoy it increasingly as he aged. He was just twenty-one when he wrote it.

All of these works for piano and orchestra consist of a single, concerto-length movement, lasting between twenty and twenty-five minutes on average, and each has its own unique form. The *Burleske* comes close to a traditional sonata structure, with clear first and second subjects, a big development, a definite recapitulation, and a madcap coda. Exactly what Strauss was making fun of remains a mystery. The original title of the piece was *Scherzo* (Joke), and the subversive element is provided by the timpanist, who, remarkably for the period, starts the piece off with a solo on four drums and interrupts regularly with positively manic glee.

The piano soloist enters frantically, with passages featuring melodramatic, chromatic harmony, before settling down to a more systematic presentation of the main themes. The overall musical style comes across as Brahms on steroids, and this too may be what annoyed Bülow—never mind Brahms himself. Although it was composed before the tone poems, many commentators regard the *Burleske* as one of Strauss' first mature compositions, and both the title and sound of the actual music suggest a programmatic backstory of some kind.

More significantly, the work is the first in which Strauss' impish sense of humor takes control and thumbs its nose at the German musical establishment. In this respect, Strauss was unique. He was on the verge of dumping Brahms as his idol and pledging allegiance to the even more humorless Wagnerians, but once he realized how good he was at comedic writing, he never looked back. The *Burleske* begins a process that would result in *Till Eulenspiegel* and *Don Quixote* in short order, and the comic operas to come as well.

Parergon zur Symphonia Domestica (1924–25)
Scoring: 2 flutes, 2 oboes, 2 clarinets, bass clarinet, 2 bassoons, contrabassoon, 4 horns, 2 trumpets, 3 trombones, tuba, harp, timpani, solo piano, strings

Panathenäenzug (1926–27)
Scoring: piccolo, 3 flutes, 2 oboes, English horn, 2 clarinets, bass clarinet, 3 bassoons, 4 horns, 3 trumpets, 3 trombones, tuba, glockenspiel, cymbals, harp, celesta, timpani, solo piano, strings

The next two works were both commissioned in the 1920s by Paul Wittgenstein, brother of the famous philosopher Ludwig, and a pianist who lost his right arm in World War I. He was not the only one: Janáček dedicated his *Capriccio* for piano left-hand and instrumental ensemble to a one-armed Czech pianist, but Wittgenstein commissioned an unprecedented set of works from numerous major composers, including Prokofiev, Britten, Korngold, Hindemith, Schmidt, Strauss, and above all Ravel. He was, in fact, a pretty dreadful pianist judging from surviving evidence. You can hear him ruin the Ravel Left-Hand Concerto in a 1937 performance from Amsterdam available on YouTube, but the world owes him a debt of gratitude for the pieces that were written for him.

Strauss was fascinated by the challenge of writing effective piano music for left hand alone. The unusual idiom combines with the unpronounceable (even in German) titles of these works to make them some of his least played and least recorded musical curiosities. Wittgenstein apparently retained exclusive rights to performances until 1950, which would have been fine had he been a great pianist who played them regularly, but he wasn't, and he didn't, so the original circumstances of their composition prevented others from trying them out. Admittedly they are strange, but once you get to know them, they prove oddly compelling too, and certainly like nothing else by Strauss or anyone else.

A *parergon* is an appendix, or ornamental addition to something larger. You can be forgiven if you can't see yourself saying to a musical friend, "Let's run over to my place and listen to my new recording of the *Parergon zur Symphonia Domestica*." It's Strauss' fault. It also doesn't help to learn that the distressed version of the baby's theme from the *Symphonia* on which the piano work is based tells the story of little Franz Strauss' battle with typhoid fever and (happily) his eventual recovery. What this has to do with the solo part is anyone's guess, but the music begins sadly and gradually "recovers" its genial demeanor. Maybe the solo represents penicillin? Sorry, that wasn't discovered until 1928. The pianist plays almost constantly throughout, both alone and as an undercurrent accompanying the orchestral discourse, and the piece overall has a most curious, bittersweet quality.

The *Panathenäenzug* isn't as tough to pronounce as it sounds: PAHN-ahten-AYen-tsoog. What it is, though, is another matter. The word means "all-Athenian procession," and it refers to the ancient Greek festival celebrating the goddess Athena, during which there were athletic contests, dancing, feasting, and a big procession to the Acropolis. So this piece belongs in the list of Strauss' "Greek" works, sort of, only it also has a purely musical subtitle: "Symphonic Etudes in Passacaglia Form," which pretty clearly describes what the music does.

A passacaglia is a set of variations over a constantly repeated theme in the bass. The most famous ones are Bach's Passacaglia and Fugue in C Minor for organ, and the finale of Brahms' Fourth Symphony. More modern examples include Britten's Passacaglia from his opera *Peter Grimes* and the slow movement of Shostakovich's First Violin Concerto. The passacaglia is quite similar to the French chaconne, and in most modern works the two terms can be used interchangeably. So the "*zug*" in the title probably refers to the steadily advancing procession of variations over the bass theme, which is presented initially pizzicato, and concludes with three quarter notes in triplet rhythm. This gives the otherwise uniformly steady notes of the theme a nice little shuffle at the end, helping the listener to mark each recurrence.

The "etude" part refers to the fact that the writing for the soloist explores everything possible for left hand, systematically, and in a symphonic context. As in the *Parergon*, the soloist plays the freakishly difficult, note-heavy piano part almost continuously, sometimes dominating the orchestra, sometimes playing alone, but just as frequently accompanying the ensemble with elaborately ornamental filigree. The overall tone of the work is brighter and more ebullient than that of its companion, in keeping with the festive theme.

The orchestra opens with a brass fanfare leading directly to a solo cadenza, and then the passacaglia begins. Lasting some twenty-five minutes in all, the first one or two dozen variations are very strict, sticking closely to the theme, which takes only eight short bars in 2/4 time; then the work begins to expand. After the first few minutes, don't expect to hear the passacaglia tune in the bass of each variation or episode. When Strauss wants you to notice it, you will. As the music proceeds, it becomes increasingly fantastic, culminating in a dreamy episode for harp, celesta, glockenspiel, and solo piano, before the orchestra wakes up and brings the work to a close with a rousing march led by the piano.

The *Panathenäenzug* is a finer, more varied work than the *Parergon*, notwithstanding which it is by far the more conspicuously neglected of the two. This may be because no one knows or cares what a *Panathenäenzug* is and can't be bothered to find out, or because the *Parergon* uses themes already familiar from its parent work and is marginally shorter and easier to play. Whatever the reason, and whether or not you can pronounce it, you should give the *Panathenäenzug* a listen. It's great fun, and sustains repetition very well.

Serenades for Wind Ensemble

Some decades ago, I was playing a concert with a community orchestra. The feature work was Respighi's *The Pines of Rome*, and in typical community orchestra fashion we had the full assemblage of winds, brass, and percussion, plus something like six violins, three violas, two cellos, and one half of a double bass. Due to the dearth of strings and excess of everything else, the conductor decided to do Strauss' "The Happy Workshop" on the first half. I was only playing in the second half (percussion) in the Respighi, and I remember thinking at the time that the Strauss was the most lethally boring forty minutes of music I had ever encountered.

That wasn't entirely fair, and with age comes wisdom. Wind serenades are not designed to be thrilling. By nature they are relaxed, easygoing, and pleasant, what the Germans call *gemütlich*, and if you adjust your expectations accordingly, you will find them very enjoyable. You can pay attention to them when the mood strikes you, and they will reward your notice, but they make terrific background music too, and there's no shame in that. After all, they originated in the "table music" meant to entertain aristocratic patrons during meals and other convivial gatherings, and they still do that admirably.

Serenade for 13 Wind Instruments, Op. 7 (1881)
Suite for 13 Wind Instruments, Op. 4 (1884)
Scoring: 2 flutes, 2 oboes, 2 clarinets, 4 horns, 2 bassoons, contrabassoon (or tuba)

Strauss' wind-ensemble music, like the horn concertos, belongs to the beginning and end of his career. The charming and mellifluous Serenade of 1881, a single movement lasting a mere eight minutes, was his first great compositional success. Smiling and unpretentious, it led to the writing of the Suite, even though the opus numbers got mixed up so that the Serenade looks like it came later. The Suite has four movements and is full of good tunes, especially the perky Gavotte, one of the most captivating quick movements in all of Strauss.

First Sonatina for 16 Wind Instruments (1943) ("From the Workshop of an Invalid")
Second Sonatina for 16 Wind Instruments (1945), a.k.a. Symphony for Wind Instruments ("The Happy Workshop")
Scoring: 2 flutes, 2 oboes, 3 clarinets, basset horn, bass clarinet, 4 horns, 2 bassoons, contrabassoon

The two late sonatinas are certainly not "little sonatas." They are very large works, and Strauss was right to call the second of them a "symphony." It lasts some forty minutes, but its predecessor is only about five minutes shorter. Strauss was recovering from the flu when he composed the First Sonatina, hence the subtitle, but the music itself is lithe and chipper. The enlarged clarinet section in these pieces gives the timbres a wonderful, fruity mellowness, and Strauss captures sonorities from this limited ensemble that are truly novel and amazingly rich.

In the First Sonatina, Strauss needed only three movements, although the finale is extremely long (about thirteen minutes). Actually, he cheated a bit: the central slow movement offers a combination of Romance and Minuet. The Wind Symphony (Sonatina No. 2) has the usual four movements, with the very long first movement and finale playing for about half an hour and the brief inner movements requiring only about four minutes each. Both are moderate in tempo. So you can clearly see that Strauss was not out to dazzle you with overt brilliance, though much of the writing is highly virtuosic. Rather, the mood is consistently easygoing, even where darker shadows fleetingly appear.

When writing the sonatinas, Strauss somewhat contemptuously referred to them as "wrist exercises," written for his own pleasure, and he forbade their publication or performance until after his death. There is no question that he composed these pieces in order to explore specific compositional challenges in working with limited ensembles. It may also be that he finally understood that no one wanted to hear cheerful evocations of a bygone classical ideal amid the rubble of postwar Europe. He had already learned that lesson the hard way, after the first world war, in connection with *Die Frau ohne Schatten* and *Schlagobers*. He was too old and disillusioned to go through that ordeal again. It was his acknowledgment, coming at the very end of his life, that even artists at some point had to bow to an external reality.

Tone Poems I
People

Strauss' tone poems tend to fall naturally into groups, offering a logical opportunity for a discussion organized by their subject matter: people, places, and things. The first group is the largest and contains works based on literary or historical characters, as well as two of Strauss' more famous autobiographical portraits. The tone poems about places similarly may be considered autobiographical to the extent that they take their cues from the composer's personal experiences, and we need to stretch the concept of "place" just a bit to include the nonspecific realm of "nature." Finally, two works embody Strauss' musings on death, mortality, and the afterlife, a tricky if popular topic for musical illustration, and one especially interesting coming from a composer who was basically an atheist or agnostic (Strauss scholars often debate this detail).

A "tone poem," as the name implies, is simply a piece of descriptive music, an illustration in tones. Although Liszt is usually credited as the inventor of the distinct genre (he called it a "symphonic poem"), descriptive or "program" music has been around forever, and therefore so has the tone-poem idea. Vivaldi's *The Four Seasons*, for example, consists of four concertos that attempt to illustrate the words of four genuine poems that preface each work. But these are also violin concertos that make perfect sense whether you know the poems or not. There are also programmatic symphonies: Beethoven's "Pastoral," Berlioz's *Symphonie fantastique* and *Harold in Italy*, and many others. So you might say that a tone poem is an illustrative piece of music that is not also something else, but as with many definitions of genre in music, the lines can get very blurry.

This fact doesn't mean that tone poems have no distinct form. The ones that have only a single movement and last less than about fifteen to twenty minutes grew out of a very well-established late eighteenth- and early nineteenth-century genre: the overture. Famous examples include Beethoven's *Egmont* and *Coriolan*, Schumann's *Manfred*, Mendelssohn's *Calm Sea and Prosperous Voyage*, *The Hebrides*, and *A Midsummer Night's Dream*, as well as operatic overtures such as Haydn's "The Representation of Chaos" from the oratorio *The Creation*, Rossini's *William Tell*, and Weber's *Der Freischütz*, among many others. As you can see from the titles, these overtures take their names from people, places, stories, or events, and they may be either highly illustrative or more generally evocative of mood. They also may be written as stand-alone works or may have entered the concert hall after originating as true theatrical preludes.

The main similarity between an overture and a single-movement tone poem, though this is by no means a hard-and-fast rule, is that both tend to take the shape of a symphonic first movement, often displaying some version of sonata form as romantic composers understood it. That means an energetic or passionate first theme; a contrasting, more lyrical second theme; a turbulent development; and a restatement (recapitulation) of the original material, often with more development depending on the trajectory of the story. There may also be an introduction and an extended coda. This may sound restrictive, but it really isn't. You would be amazed at just how many stories can be squeezed into this format with complete naturalness.

Consider Tchaikovsky's *Romeo and Juliet*, which he called an overture but which everyone since has regarded as a symphonic poem. There's an introduction (Friar Lawrence), a first theme (battle music), a lyrical second theme (the famous love music for Romeo and Juliet), and a development in which all of these get combined in very dramatic fashion, leading to an even more intense recapitulation, where the love music gets swallowed up in the violent battle, leading to the death (timpani roll) of Romeo and Juliet. A sad coda wraps up the story. The reason sonata form works so well in these circumstances is that it is in itself dramatic: its themes enact a story over the course of a musical argument of some length, and it doesn't matter whether we consider the tunes as representing specific characters or treat them abstractly, as capturing more generalized feelings and emotions.

Strauss' tone poems differ from earlier examples of the genre, not so much in purpose as in sheer size and musical ambition. They are bigger, longer, more glamorous, and also more avowedly illustrative and full of incident than any previous examples of the form. In order to sustain their greater length and range of expression, Strauss was forced to create his own approach to form, which may seem intimidating but really is not. Virtually all musical form in the classical and romantic periods boils down to three basic and relatively simple procedures: (1) the sonata principle just described; (2) a series of variations on a single theme; and (3) what has come to be known as song form (ABA) or, when stretched out, "rondo" or "ritornello" form (ABACADA, etc.).

No matter how intricately Strauss or any other tonal composer of the period extends his musical argument, at its core you will hear these basic principles either alone or in some combination, adapted to the matter at hand. There is quite literally no avoiding them if the music is to have a satisfying, audible shape. Otherwise the result will be the extreme boredom produced by a work that seems to go nowhere and do nothing with its material, however attractive it may sound initially.

The reason, then, that I begin this discussion of the tone poems with matters of form is simple: no successful piece of program music survives on how illustrative it actually is—if by this we mean how much the noise that it makes reminds us of something extramusical. Even a totally illustrative piece like Mussorgsky's *Pictures at an Exhibition*—a suite of short, self-contained vignettes describing actual paintings and drawings—depends for much of its success on the purely musical ordering of its parts, to say nothing of the "Promenade" tune that returns at critical points, rondo-like, and imposes a larger shape on the whole. What makes Strauss' tone poems so fascinating, then, is not so much that they successfully illustrate their subjects, but rather how they do it; and that means investigating their form. After all, if the only thing that matters is the "story," then there's no point in further inquiry.

There is another very good justification to talk about matters of form in considering the tone poems: Strauss himself asks us to. This aspect mattered to him every bit as much as the descriptive element.

Till Eulenspiegel is described as a work in "rondeau" form, and Strauss goes so far as to use the French term (as opposed to the normal Italian "rondo"), thereby driving musicologists crazy ever after in trying to figure out what he meant. *Don Quixote* is a set of "variations on a theme of knightly character," while two of the tone poems are called "symphonies." So as you can see, questions of form are very important, as well as very interesting in their own right.

During Strauss' lifetime, the premieres of the tone poems often were accompanied by detailed booklets that allegedly revealed what each musical episode attempts to describe. This made sense in the days before recordings, when a single audition might be one's only chance to hear music full of strange and evocative new sounds. All questions of form and other purely musical issues aside, our approach must be somewhat different for a couple of reasons.

First, much of the music's sheer sonic shock value has long worn off and does not need to be explained or justified. Second, there are times when an excess of specificity can be downright harmful. While it's great to know what the music supposedly represents—and we will by no means neglect this aspect of it in the discussion that follows—it's just as important to understand that if you don't hear what you are supposed to, there is no reason to conclude that the work is a failure or there is something wrong with your own perceptions. Each listener's personal impressions and subjective perceptions are valid and legitimate answers to the question of what any piece of music expresses.

The degree to which music can describe a person, place, object, or event, and still succeed on purely musical terms, is an incredibly interesting subject. It has served as a source of controversy throughout musical history. Each Strauss tone poem asks this question in a different way and proposes a unique answer. Exploring this aspect of the music in light of the work's stated program inevitably leads to a richer experience, one that rewards the sort of repetition that home listening to recordings allows. This, for me, represents a major aspect of the music's enduring appeal. It is time now to take a closer look.

Literary Characters: Macbeth, Don Juan, Till Eulenspiegel, and Don Quixote

Macbeth (1888–91)

Scoring: piccolo, 3 flutes, 2 oboes, English horn, 2 clarinets, bass clarinet, 2 bassoons, contrabassoon, 4 horns, 3 trumpets, bass trumpet, 3 trombones, tuba, cymbals, tam-tam, bass drum, snare drum, timpani, strings

Macbeth is the first of Strauss' one-movement tone poems, as well as the darkest and most violent, in keeping with the tenor of Shakespeare's play. Its relative lack of popularity stems largely from the fact that it has none of the luscious, erotic musical element for which Strauss is rightly acclaimed, nor does it offer much relief from the gloom and doom of the story. It is in fact admirably concentrated. This only goes to show that a piece of program music that sticks too closely to the story runs the risk of being a narrative success and a musical failure. *Macbeth* is not a musical failure, but it took Strauss a while to figure out exactly how it needed to go.

Originally the work concluded with a triumphal march for Macduff, but then Hans von Bülow asked Strauss, effectively, "Who cares about Macduff in a tone poem called *Macbeth*?" Taking this very sensible advice to heart, Strauss revised the ending in a way that has nothing to do with the play, and everything to do with tone poetry. As you can hear for yourself, the piece now ends with a ghostly reminder of the work's main themes, representing Macbeth and Lady Macbeth respectively, supported by distant snare-drum rolls. It's a wholly appropriate and satisfying conclusion to a work that does not deserve its neglect in concert, even if Strauss never wrote anything else quite like it again.

Formally speaking, *Macbeth* is very easy to follow, being written almost in textbook sonata form, with striking pauses or clear changes of texture between sections. Strauss even names the main material "Macbeth" and "Lady Macbeth," and offers a quotation from Shakespeare over the music for the latter. Here is an outline of the form:

Exposition

First theme: Macbeth, an angry orchestral outburst, with a prominent, gloomy theme on the cellos and basses that will become
increasingly important as the music proceeds.

Second theme: Lady Macbeth, a sweet melody on flutes and clarinets,
interspersed with anxious outbursts.

Development

First part: The themes of Macbeth and Lady Macbeth alternate in
increasingly tense dialogue, as if she is goading him to murder
Duncan (the king), which likely occurs at the big cymbal crash,
followed by an insanely fast and difficult flurry from the full
string section.

Second part: Macbeth's themes are transformed into a noble march.
He has become the king. This rises to a grand climax.

Recapitulation

First theme: Reprise of Macbeth.

Second theme: Reprise of Lady Macbeth, now a ghostly shadow of
her former self. Indeed, you might not recognize her at first. Is
this her mad scene?

Coda (Second Development Section)

First part: A huge and tragic climax, capped by bass drum, cymbals,
and multiple crashes on the tam-tam (which most performances
severely underplay—the best version features Neeme Järvi conducting the Royal Scottish National Orchestra on the Chandos
label).

Second part: The sepulchral conclusion featuring fragments of the
main themes colored by offstage snare-drum rolls, leading to the
angry final gesture.

Macbeth illustrates very pointedly some of the principal issues that
Strauss had to deal with in setting Shakespeare's drama to music.
Practically the entire first half of the work focuses on the two main
characters. It describes them, but from a narrative point of view nothing happens until the death of Duncan, if that indeed is what the first
half of the development section represents (it hardly could be anything

else). After that, Strauss has a real problem, because Shakespeare's play contains a lot of action: the murder of Banquo and the return of his ghost, Lady Macbeth's sleepwalking scene and her death, the final battle and death of Macbeth, and let's not forget the witches.

If the first half of the tone poem is quite specific, the second half leaves much more to the listener's imagination. The witches, clearly, play no part. It is difficult also to imagine Banquo's contribution to the proceedings. Bülow surely was correct to tell Strauss to forget about following the story and concentrate his efforts on the powerful characters he had illustrated in the exposition. And so Macbeth's music returns even more turbulently; Lady Macbeth's disintegrates, presumably as her mind does, and all we know about what happens afterward is that the music depicts events of extreme violence, followed by Macbeth's death and a hint of returned calm just before the end. Shakespeare's exact dramatic succession of events is less important than a balanced and succinct musical form.

The other aspect of *Macbeth* that is worth keeping in mind in almost all of the works that follow is the idea of "development," and specifically, the "development section" of a movement in first-movement sonata form. One of Strauss' great innovations, formally speaking, was his discovery that he could put the development section (or sections, if there is more than one) just about anywhere, with very different results each time. In *Macbeth*, it occurs where you would expect it to: in the middle, although there is also a great deal of further development at the end in what is technically the coda. This is not new: both Haydn and Beethoven wrote large codas that are effectively second development sections, as Strauss well knew.

Just to be clear, by "development," we mean a highly contrasted passage, usually in quick tempo, that transforms existing material in a limitless number of ways but that may also include episodes based on entirely new themes. It is different from mere "variation," in that it gives a strong feeling of forward movement, rapid change, or transformation—in short, of dramatic events happening in real time. It often leads to a restatement of the main themes in their original form or key, thus providing a definite sense of arrival at a long-foreseen goal. Spotting the development section offers a very useful way of understanding a

movement's form more generally, especially when the music purports
to tell a story, because it's where much of the action happens.

Don Juan (1888)

Scoring: piccolo, 3 flutes, 2 oboes, English horn, 2 clarinets, 2 bassoons, contra-
bassoon, 4 horns, 3 trumpets, 3 trombones, tuba, triangle, glockenspiel, cymbals,
timpani, harp, strings

Programmatically speaking, you can expect to find development sections wherever Strauss tries to describe the interactions of one or
more of his musical characters: in battles, parties, storms, love scenes,
quarrels, and the like. In the tone poem that he composed more or less
contemporaneously with *Macbeth*, *Don Juan* (CD Track 1), there is a
central party scene that clearly represents the development section (at
10:10). However, if this particular part of the movement remains in the
usual spot, the other parts reveal some very surprising features. *Don
Juan* is usually considered Strauss' first masterpiece of tone poetry, and
one of the reasons has to do with its perfection of form, not because
it is unusually strict, but because in this work Strauss has set himself
free by selecting a narrative particularly suitable to musical treatment.

The *Don Juan* story is well known, primarily from Mozart's opera
Don Giovanni; Strauss' tone poem is based on an unfinished verse drama
by German nineteenth-century writer Nikolaus Lenau. The musical
advantage of this story is its simplicity: Don Juan meets and beds a
number of women, and at the end his misdeeds lead to his death, usually by getting sucked down to hell (Mozart) or in a duel (Lenau). All
of the other details of the legend, including the number and kind of
his amorous conquests, can differ at will. This gives Strauss complete
freedom in his treatment of the story, and in listening it's actually better
to forget about Lenau entirely. The program might as well as have been
Strauss' proprietary invention.

Before considering the music in more detail, it's worthwhile to take
a moment to look at the orchestration as compared to *Macbeth*. Missing
from the wind section of *Don Juan* is the bass clarinet, and the percussion features bright, high-pitched instruments (triangle, glockenspiel,
cymbals), whereas *Macbeth* asks for the darker sonorities of bass drum,

tam-tam, and snare drum (aside from cymbals). *Don Juan*, appropriately, makes extensive use of the harp; *Macbeth* omits the instrument entirely. Outwardly these appear to be small differences, but their impact is profound, particularly since Strauss takes pains to color each work precisely with these disparate sonorities. So if *Macbeth* accordingly sounds dark and violent, *Don Juan* is largely bright and brilliant, indeed shockingly so. The music glitters.

Like all of the tone poems about people, *Don Juan* begins with a sketch of the main character—dashing, young, brash—with rushing strings, brass fanfares, and rhythmic volleys between the triangle and glockenspiel. The music surges irresistibly forward until the Don spies his prey. A rapid flirtation ensues, but this passage merely acts as a transition to the point where the Don's gaze alights upon The One. The orchestra comes to a full stop (1:36) on a chord that can only be described as "sexy." Harp, glockenspiel, and solo violin tell us all we need to know about the object of the Don's affections. The ensuing love scene offers listeners the first sample of Strauss in full-blown erotic mode, and a graphic moment it certainly is.

No sooner does it end, though, than Don Juan is off to pursue his next encounter. Some commentators regard this varied repetition of the opening as the start of the formal development section. Others view it, and Love Scene No. 2 (a blissful nocturne in slow tempo featuring a delicious theme for solo oboe at 6:15), as the second part of a double exposition, such as we sometimes hear in classical concerto first movements, where the orchestra introduces the main themes alone, followed by the solo and orchestra together. Frankly, neither of these explanations comports with the musical facts, for reasons that will become clear very shortly.

The standard form that this opening most resembles is that of a rondo (ABACA etc.), except that immediately following the second love scene a splendid new theme appears, triumphantly intoned by the horns (at 9:20). It unmistakably belongs to Don Juan, and it initiates what is clearly a development section (a masked ball in the original play) in which the previous characters all rub shoulders in music of extreme gaiety. Perhaps the horn motive represents the Don in his party costume. Either way, the development leads inexorably to a recapitulation of the work's opening. Now Strauss faces a formal problem that he solves with what can only be called genius.

Having returned to the music of Don Juan the adventurous lecher, what will Strauss use as his "second subject"? The entire point of the Don's amorous wanderings is that once he conquers his prize, he never returns to her again. That effectively rules out the music of both of the preceding love scenes. Instead, Strauss chooses as his second subject (at 13:35) the horn tune of the "masked Don." This melody does in fact bear a general rhythmic resemblance to that of the first love scene, and as sung out by the strings it feels incredibly natural in its present position.

So what began like a rondo turns out to be a kind of sonata-form movement after all, except that the formal, two-subject exposition appears at the very end. Not only does this stand the textbook form on its head, it is entirely consistent with the portrait of Don Juan as a seducer and narcissist who abandons his women as soon as they yield to him. There is no inconsistency between Strauss' program and its musical embodiment. Indeed, you could probably figure out what was happening in the music without knowing anything of its program at all. It's that clear and vivid.

Don Juan succeeds, then, because it has enough of the structural endowments of traditional forms to give the music the shape that it needs (and drive subsequent generations of commentators crazy trying to explain the piece in conventional terms), but also a freedom and originality of treatment that really does recall the music of the classical masters. For them, the later formal categories and strictures of the romantic period obviously did not exist, and each work presented new challenges surmounted by unique solutions.

The conclusion of *Don Juan* is shocking. As already noted, in the play the Don gets killed in a duel, not because he is losing, but because at that moment he realizes the pointlessness and futility of his life, and so he allows himself to be run through by his opponent's sword. Strauss, again shrewdly, does not try to imitate the deathblow, which would not have been difficult. Music is full of "bang-splat" death portrayals, the most famous probably being the "crash-plonk-plonk" of the guillotined head rolling into the basket in Berlioz's *Symphonie fantastique*. Rather,

Strauss concentrates on Don Juan's psychological state of total disgust. The music reaches its most powerful climax, cuts off, and then with cold, minor-key harmonies shudders abruptly to a close, rejecting all that had come before with a dismissive shrug. It's at once disturbing and, somehow, inevitable.

In considering *Macbeth* and *Don Juan* you may notice a pattern beginning to emerge. Both end with the death of the protagonist, and both seek to find a musical shape that permits Strauss to portray a series of incidents along the way to that tragic (or at all events fatal) resolution. *Don Juan* is special in that those incidents are essentially all of the same kind—love scenes—and the problems that Strauss encountered in determining the final form of *Macbeth* basically stem from the need to boil down the very complex plot into a series of musically comprehensible and logically continuous episodes.

Till Eulenspiegels Lustige Streiche (Till Eulenspiegel's Merry Pranks) (1894–95)

Scoring: piccolo, 3 flutes, 3 oboes, English horn, 3 clarinets, bass clarinet, 3 bassoons, contrabassoon, 8 horns, 6 trumpets, 3 trombones, tuba, 4 timpani, bass drum, snare drum, cymbals, triangle, large ratchet (cog rattle), strings

In his next tone poem about a literary character, *Till Eulenspiegel's Merry Pranks*, Strauss faced a similar problem, but he had the advantage of being able to select from a wide range of incidents without having to worry about the result being compared to a classic play whose plot would be familiar to most educated listeners. Till Eulenspiegel (the last name means "owl mirror") was a quasihistorical figure who may have lived at the beginning of the fourteenth century in northern Germany. There are numerous legends about his exploits, and not only did Strauss have his pick of the lot, he was very dodgy about detailing exactly which ones he chose. This did not prevent detailed programs describing the work's action from appearing, some with Strauss' sanction, but as you will see they are as much a hindrance as they are a help.

Till Eulenspiegel is Strauss' shortest tone poem, his funniest piece of music in any form, and his most formally complex. It is hellishly difficult to play, on account of its tricky use of rhythm and rapid changes of pace and texture, and it lasts a scant fifteen minutes in most performances. The German sense of humor also takes some getting used to. You may well ask what's so funny about Till's merry trial and happy hanging at the end, however amusingly Strauss portrays it in tones, but the coda suggests that the spirit of Till lives on past his sad demise, and the whole thing shouldn't be taken too seriously.

Strauss called *Till* a "rondo," a form that is supposed to be a simple "verse and refrain" structure: usually ABACA, but capable of infinite extension through the addition of more "verses," or episodes, between recurrences of the main theme, which in musical parlance is called a "ritornello" for the obvious reason that it keeps returning after each episode. Complications ensue because the ritornello contains at least four distinct ideas that not only may or may not return when they formally ought to, but are also substantially varied throughout the work, while bits of them also appear in the various episodes. This blurs the distinction between what is an episode and what is the refrain until close to the end, when Strauss ties the whole structure together by offering some welcome literal repetition.

If all of this sounds slightly bewildering, just keep in mind that it's all part of Strauss' plan to keep the listener off balance and eagerly anticipating Till's next move, and it works very well indeed. There is no problem at all in following the course of the action, and whether or not the bit you are listening to belongs to an episode or a variation of the ritornello isn't important at all. The key to unraveling the form, if you're curious, is simply to remember that what sounds like one of Till's adventures does not have to be an episode of the rondo form, but may in fact be a varied return of the main theme(s).

The tone poem opens with a nostalgic idea that everyone has always agreed embodies the idea of "Once upon a time." The first four notes are very important, and in fact fit the German for "Once upon a time" ("Es war einmal") perfectly. Next come three ideas all associated with the character of Till Eulenspiegel: his famous horn theme, twice repeated in full, and quickly rising to a grandiose climax; an insolent sneer on the woodwinds that's as close a musical representation of "giving someone the finger" as anyone has yet devised; and finally a short passage in galloping rhythm the perhaps represents Till on the move.

These four motives and themes, freely interspersed with new material as necessary, form the basis of the following generally accepted narrative, and I indicate how each fits into the basic rondo form as either an "episode" or an appearance of the "ritornello":

- Episode: Till causes havoc in the marketplace (cue for a giant ratchet [cog rattle] in the percussion department)
- Ritornello: Till disguised as a priest (a gracious string melody based on the galloping tune and not sounding obviously like a parody of priestly anything, at least to me)
- Episode: A lovely girl (solo violin) catches Till's eye
- Ritornello: Till flirts with the girl and, evidently, flaunts his machismo (based on the horn theme, which soon reappears)
- Episode: Pompous entry of the academics (that German sense of humor again), initially on the bassoons, culminating in . . .
- Ritornello: Till gives them the musical middle finger on woodwinds and muted brass
- Episode: Then a lighthearted, dance-like interruption before . . .
- Ritornello: The return of the horn theme and the opening climax in more or less original form

Strauss packs all of the above into about ten minutes of music. Notice that the ritornellos all represent some aspect of Till himself, even in substantially varied form, which makes sense, because that is whom the initial, principal themes purport to illustrate. The episodes, on the other hand, introduce the secondary characters or events.

The final appearance of the ritornello leads directly to one of those development-type episodes that you will find in all of these tone poems. It combines just about all of the "Till" themes and motives in brilliant, chattering counterpoint, in a manner very similar to the procedure already described in *Don Juan*. The climax features the "Till as a priest" theme, thereby confirming that it belonged to him from the beginning. An ominous snare-drum roll introduces the judgment scene, which serves simultaneously as a development of the "middle finger" motive—Till dissing the court. A couple of blasts on the brass pronounce the death sentence, and a screaming clarinet graphically illustrates Till's happy hanging.

Notice that Strauss omitted the "Once upon a time" opening from the final, nearly literal repetition of the ritornello. This is because he has saved it for this coda, where it completes the form and concludes the piece with perfect logic. It serves as a sweet reminder of, and return to, the original nostalgic atmosphere. The very last word, though, goes to Till himself. Although he may be dead in body, his rambunctious spirit lives on forever in musical legend.

With *Till Eulenspiegel's Merry Pranks*, Strauss turned loose a musical sense of humor that had appeared fitfully in previous works, such as his *Burleske* for piano and orchestra and *Don Juan* (the party scene particularly). Nothing is more controversial in music than humor, and it was even more so in late nineteenth-century Germany, where art was considered holy and musical politics was dominated by the ongoing battle between Brahmsian classicists and Wagnerian revolutionaries. The only thing the two sides had in common was their utter lack of any sense of humor, particularly the ironic humor at which Strauss excelled. Works such as *Till Eulenspiegel*, so polished and advanced in technique, yet so subversive in content, established Strauss as both Germany's greatest composer as well as the "bad boy" of modern music. They did wonders for his reputation.

Don Quixote (1897)

Scoring: piccolo, 2 flutes, 2 oboes, English horn, 2 clarinets, E-flat clarinet, bass clarinet, 3 bassoons, contrabassoon, 6 horns, 3 trumpets, 3 trombones, tenor tuba, bass tuba, cymbals, bass drum, snare drum, triangle, glockenspiel, tambourine, wind machine, timpani, harp, 16 first violins, 16 second violins, 12 violas, 10 cellos, 8 basses

Strauss' final literary character sketch, *Don Quixote*, resembles *Till Eulenspiegel* in that the original source, though better known, offered Strauss total freedom to choose those episodes that he felt most comfortable setting to music. Unlike the earlier work, however, *Don*

Quixote is a full-length essay, playing for about forty minutes, or as long as a romantic symphony. It also features substantial solo parts for the cello, representing Don Quixote, as well as the viola and tenor tuba, which combine to portray his sidekick, Sancho Panza. Dulcinea, the lady of the Don's dreams, finds her musical image in a lovely tune for solo oboe. Indeed, throughout these tone poems Strauss often reserves solo oboe and solo violin for his female characterizations.

The presence of all of these solo instruments, especially the cello, gives the work the feel of a concerto, and most of the world's most famous cellists have taken on the very challenging solo part for their instrument. However, *Don Quixote* is not a concerto, even though it continues Strauss' attempts to find new uses for classical forms. The work takes the shape of an introduction, presentation of the themes of Don Quixote and Sancho, ten variations, and a coda. The concerto element combined with a piece in variation form has plenty of classical precedents, from the finales of some of Mozart's most popular piano concertos (Nos. 17 and 24) to freestanding works such as Liszt's *Totentanz* and Franck's *Symphonic Variations*, both for piano and orchestra. Tchaikovsky's elegant *Rococo Variations* for cello and orchestra directly anticipates Strauss in the choice of solo instrument.

If *Don Quixote* is not the largest set ever written of *concertante variations* (i.e., variations for solo and orchestra as in a concerto), it is certainly the biggest work of its kind in the standard repertoire. However, if the presence of multiple soloists plus orchestra pressed into the service of variation form makes you nervous or seems to promise a work as complex as *Till Eulenspiegel*, only three times longer, don't worry. It's a fundamental rule in musical composition that the longer a piece of music is, the simpler its large-scale form tends to be—assuming the composer knows what he is doing. This is because the whole scheme of contrasts needs to be bolder, more colorful, and more memorable so that the listener can follow the argument over an extended timespan.

No musical form is easier in this respect than the theme and variations, since the fact that variations are happening in the first place is often a technical matter that need not concern us at all. When we are supposed to recognize the theme(s), we will. Otherwise it makes no difference. You simply listen from point to point as each variation unfolds in contrast to the others. This is particularly true of *Don Quixote*, which plays out as a series of monologues and dialogues between the soloists, set against the fantastical background provided by Strauss' iridescent orchestration. Each variation is like a miniature tone poem in which the principal characters react to their environment and to each other, at times almost seeming to speak. The music conveys the general emotional intensity, mood, and atmosphere of each episode, but the details—save where the tone painting is very specific—are left up to your imagination.

Although cast as a theme and variations, *Don Quixote* does contain a substantial symphonic development section in about the most unexpected place possible: right at the beginning. The work starts with a lengthy introduction depicting the Don's gradual descent into insanity. Placing the development at the beginning is crazy both formally, since there has been nothing presented that needs to develop, and programmatically, so it's a particularly appropriate and amusing opening gambit on Strauss' part. Beginning with an anticipation of what will become Don Quixote's main theme (the opening woodwind fanfare, especially, appears in many of the variations), followed by Dulcinea's melody on oboe and harp, the music becomes increasing busy and confused. To make the music sound even stranger, Strauss keeps all of the brass, and later the strings, muted to produce a distorted timbre. Recurring fanfares hint at the Don's warped conception of chivalry and knightly daring, until a final climax backed by cymbal crashes brings the music to a sudden halt and the cello announces the main theme.

Don Quixote is both Strauss' most unapologetically illustrative tone poem, as well as the one that most directly probes the boundaries of what music can and cannot express. You don't need to have read Cervantes' novel to follow the music—although it's a classic and a great wonder unto itself—but it does help at least to have a "Cliffs Notes" or, in these days, Wikipedia version in mind. More importantly, the key to any work in variation form is to know the theme(s). Both Don Quixote's and Sancho's themes are full of distinct rhythmic figures that are easily recognizable whenever they appear. The Don's theme, after its initial fanfare and a series of lyrical phrases, comes to a full close with a phrase consisting of a woodwind arabesque (on the clarinet initially) followed by three long notes, the gesture then repeated with different harmonization. Sancho follows immediately after on tenor tuba and viola, and his tune consists of a four-note "turn" preceding a chain of tiny, two-note cells with the accent always on the first, longer note. Dulcinea's oboe melody from the introduction also threads its way through many of the variations as the Don's image of ultimate beauty.

The episodes that Strauss illustrates in his variations include:

Variation 1: Jousting with windmills. I have to confess that I find it difficult to hear the windmill here, though the musical gesture—a repeated descending phrase—representing it is clear, and the point where the Don gets swatted and knocked on his backside is obvious enough. Does it sound "windmillish" to you?

Variation 2: Battle with the army of sheep. This variation offers perhaps *the* classic example of avant-garde music dressed up as comedy. The flutter-tonguing woodwinds and brass and freakishly dissonant harmonies all became standard techniques in later music, and they do indeed make a convincing herd of sheep. Strauss would never dare use such sounds in a German symphony of the period, but here the program gives him license to break new musical ground.

Variation 3: Questions and answers between the Don and Sancho. This very long variation (around eight minutes, usually) culminates in a gorgeous vision of Dulcinea.

Variation 4: Don Quixote takes on a group of penitents, who are quite identifiable through music reminiscent of Gregorian chant.

Variation 5: Don Quixote's vigil—a beautiful meditation for the solo cello, with a rhapsodic recollection of Dulcinea worked into the long melodic lines.

Variation 6: The Don mistakes a crude peasant girl for Dulcinea, with a little help from Sancho. Two oboes play a "pop"-tune parody of Dulcinea's theme, starting with Sancho's melodic turn and backed by the tambourine. The Don is furious.

Variation 7: The flight through the air (cue for the wind machine). Most discussions of this variation claim that Strauss not only illustrates flight, but also, by keeping the bass fixed on a single note, creates a "fake flight" that never actually takes off. I don't hear it, and I think the verbal description goes beyond what music audibly can do. Flight, yes; flight without ever leaving the ground, no, although it's a nice psychological point.

Variation 8: An unfortunate voyage in an enchanted boat that capsizes and leaves Don Quixote and Sancho dripping wet.

Variation 9: The Don takes on two bassoons—er, monks—who he believes are evil magicians.

Variation 10: The Duel: Don Quixote's defeat at the hands of another knight finally shatters his delusions and restores his sanity. He returns home sadly, humble as a shepherd (the pastoral woodwind music from Variation 2 returns briefly).

Coda: Death of Don Quixote, with a final, gentle recapitulation of the main themes.

Don Quixote is widely regarded as the finest of all the tone poems, the one in which form and content are most perfectly harmonious and where humor and pathos exist in perfect balance. Strauss counters the tendency of the variation format to break up into disconnected bits with both his natural melodic fluency and a careful arrangement of the individual episodes to maximize coherence while offering a wide range of musical contrasts. The concertante writing for cello and viola/tenor tuba, as well as the Dulcinea theme, also provides a unifying thread that binds the entire work together effortlessly. You may have noticed that all of these works end with the death of the protagonist, a conscious choice for Strauss, who regarded them all as a sort of practice for the operas to come. Writing a good death scene is the stock-in-trade of any serious would-be opera composer, and there will be a couple more in this survey.

Strauss' Self-Portraits: *A Hero's Life* and *Symphonia Domestica*

Ein Heldenleben (A Hero's Life) (1898)

Scoring: piccolo, 3 flutes, 4 oboes, English horn, 3 clarinets, bass clarinet, 3 bassoons, contrabassoon, 8 horns, 5 trumpets, 3 trombones, tenor tuba, bass tuba, timpani, bass drum, cymbals, small snare drum, large tenor drum, tam-tam, triangle, 16 first and 16 second violins, 12 violas, 12 cellos, 8 basses, 2 harps

Strauss considered *Ein Heldenleben* to be a companion piece to *Don Quixote*, which was written at about the same time. Both works treat the subject of a comic antihero, but in the case of the later work the protagonist is Strauss himself, and the comedy rests not so much on the specific actions illustrated, but in the mock seriousness with which Strauss treats the program in the first place. The idea of using music to illustrate the life and career of a composer was not new, but making him a full-blown, larger-than-life character going to battle against his atonal enemies, the critics, in a sort of autobiographical epic certainly was provocative. Furthermore, *Ein Heldenleben* shares its principal key, E-flat major, with that of Beethoven's "Eroica" Symphony, one of Strauss' favorite works. He was well aware that connoisseurs and professionals would note the allusion.

It would appear, then, that Strauss had every intention of sticking a dagger into the philosophical heart of what had become a terribly serious and aesthetically stifling aspect of German musical culture, namely, the belief in the romantic "artist-as-hero" that Beethoven's symphony essentially inaugurated and that Wagner's music ratified. Paradoxically, no one had a more passionate certainty of the superiority of German musical culture than did Strauss, but he also saw clearly that the concept of the Wagnerian artist-hero, with all of its philosophical baggage and idealistic theories of social transformation through music, was a dead end, leading to the production of endless quantities of poor imitation Wagner. Strauss idolized Wagner the composer, but he despised "Wagnerism" the cult. No work of his says this more clearly than *Ein*

Heldenleben, in which Strauss employs the full Wagnerian orchestral apparatus in order to elevate and celebrate the ordinary in the most heroic possible terms.

The program of *Ein Heldenleben* is Strauss' own, but he omitted it from the published score and it is quite possible that some of it remains undisclosed, especially after the battle, where matters become a bit blurry, illustratively speaking. The music plays continuously for about forty-five minutes and falls into eight or nine well-defined sections, depending on how you count them. Tradition assigns these episodes the following titles, which I elaborate very slightly to follow the actual course of the music more closely:

1. The Hero
2. The Hero's Enemies (The Critics)
3. The Hero's Companion
4. Love Scene (First Development Section)
5. Battle Against the Critics (Second Development Section)
6. The Hero Victorious (Recapitulation)
7. The Hero's Works of Peace (a.k.a. Strauss' Greatest Hits)
8. Disillusionment at Life
9. Withdrawal from the World, Recollection of Past Struggles, and Peaceful Death

The above program raises some curious issues that have no clear solutions but that require a bit of further discussion. Specifically, what is the point of those last three sections, and especially the disillusionment, withdrawal, and death business? After all, the hero has won the battle, beaten his critics, and gotten the girl, and he ought to be happy. Consequently, many listeners feel that the work is too long. The "works of peace" can be justified as a sort of recapitulation substitute for the now-vanquished critics, giving listeners a taste of what they had been criticizing, but the hero's disgust with life appears particularly unmotivated. By rights, the music should end triumphantly after the battle, particularly as it seems to be heading in that direction as a result of the clear recapitulation of the hero's opening themes. However, like *Don Quixote*, the story concludes in resignation and death.

Consequently, the work not only looks too long programmatically, it very easily *sounds* too long in an uninspired performance. The majority of these tone poems essentially "play themselves," in the sense that they can take a lot of grief from less-than-sympathetic conductors and still convince on account of their tight construction and sheer orchestral splendor. Not this one. It needs a sensitive interpretation, particularly as regards pacing, and many if not most modern performances are simply too slow and heavy. There are more bad recordings of *Ein Heldenleben* than of any other Strauss tone poem, without question. This is all the more puzzling when we consider that Strauss was not constrained by a preexisting literary program, but created his own and thus had complete freedom in determining the most effective musical structure.

Perhaps part of the problem stems from the inevitable change in focus that occurs in the last two sections, which can't be autobiographical at all since Strauss, who was in his mid-thirties when he wrote *Ein Heldenleben*, hadn't lived them yet. So they can come across as somewhat contrived. The work purports to encompass the hero's entire life, obliging Strauss to extrapolate into his own future—a curiously sad one, as it turns out, but one consistent (as we shall see) with the Nietzschean worldview depicted in *Also sprach Zarathustra* and *An Alpine Symphony*.

I dwell on this issue now because *Ein Heldenleben* represents the first appearance of a musical habit that will become almost the rule in later Strauss, the operas especially: the music continues well past the most logical point where it should have ended. In the operas, this means that the plot stops while the singers just get out there and sing, sometimes for quite a while. This reluctance to draw the music to a definitive close at the most logical point may or may not be a defect, depending both on your point of view and on how wonderful the remaining music sounds, but there's no getting around it. Does this suggest that Strauss may have been, in his heart of hearts, a composer of "absolute" music after all, or did he just have a defective sense of timing? There is no answer, and listeners must decide for themselves, taking each case as it comes.

Whatever qualms the work raises as to its final form, *Ein Heldenleben* offers a rich smorgasbord of brilliant music and vivid characterization, with melodies consistently out of Strauss' top drawer. If you are familiar with the tone poems already discussed, then you will recognize the particular "Straussian" features of the themes here. That of the hero rises and falls over a huge range (try singing it), similar to Till Eulenspiegel's horn tune. The critics' atonal chattering on the woodwinds offers Strauss yet another opportunity to write modern, dissonant music in a humorous vein, much like the sheep in *Don Quixote*. Pay special attention to the mysterious four-note motive in the tubas. It will return later, suggesting that not all the forces of evil have been vanquished and igniting the hero's disillusionment.

In another nod to *Don Quixote*, a solo violin, in what becomes a genuine concerto movement, takes the part of the hero's companion. Strauss himself said that he had tried to capture the capricious personality of his wife, Pauline. The love scene harkens back to *Don Juan*, and it ends with the same cadence theme that Strauss used to conclude the section "Of Those in the Back-World" in *Also sprach Zarathustra*. Offstage trumpets announce the impending battle with muted fanfares, while the battle itself, the work's principal development section, graphically describes the conflict between the hero and his adversaries, while Pauline looks on anxiously from the sidelines. It's delightfully cartoonish.

As the battle grinds to a halt, the hero scoops up his ladylove and Strauss returns to his opening theme in all of its original, surging confidence. The triumph grows in amplitude, culminating in the horn call from *Don Juan*, followed immediately by that work's first love theme. The music coasts to a halt, and the enemy tubas hint at the disillusionment to come before launching "The Hero's Works of Peace," a substantial polyphonic fantasy on themes from most of Strauss' previous major works. The more you know them, the more you can hear, but it's not necessary to have any familiarity at all to enjoy the music, which suggests an oasis of productive tranquility. This section rises to a climax followed by a pause, and a failed effort to continue that evaporates into the gentle rippling of the two harps.

Now the tubas try again, and this time disillusionment grips the hero with furiously rushing strings and snarling brass. This is really vicious music, but the storm soon passes as under throbbing timpani we hear one of those pastoral motives on the English horn that accompanied the sheep in *Don Quixote*, and also his sad journey home to die. This sound clearly had significance to Strauss as a symbol of nature, simplicity, and perhaps peace. It will return in *An Alpine Symphony* as well. The final, valedictory section begins with a descending violin melody reminiscent of a sunset. Even here, Strauss reserves one last recollection of the battle before the hero dies peacefully, his companion by his side. Originally the work ended in this manner, softly, evaporating into thin air, but Strauss later added the final crescendo and gradual diminuendo for the brass and percussion as a more fittingly heroic conclusion.

As this description suggests, *Ein Heldenleben* is not a series of disconnected episodes. The theme of the hero runs through all of them, and particularly after the formal development of the battle there is a continued intermingling of the principal ideas even though the "action" has ended and the focus has shifted to the hero alone. This, along with the revised ending, suggests that Strauss was aware of the need to firm up the musical structure in the work's later stages, even to the detriment of programmatic clarity.

Symphonia Domestica (1903)
Scoring: piccolo, 3 flutes, 2 oboes, oboe d'amore, English horn, 4 clarinets, bass clarinet, 4 bassoons, contrabassoon, 4 saxophones, 8 horns, 4 trumpets, 3 trombones, tuba, timpani, triangle, tambourine, glockenspiel, cymbals, bass drum, 16 first and 16 second violins, 12 violas, 10 cellos, 8 basses, 2 harps

No such concerns plague the *Symphonia Domestica*, a musical day in the life of Strauss, his wife, and his infant son, Franz. As with all of the larger tone poems, the structure is quite simple in outline, however richly elaborated: (1) Introduction and Scherzo, (2) Adagio, (3) Fugue and Finale. The piece lasts for about forty to forty-five minutes and plays continuously.

That's really all there is to it—three sections of roughly comparable size, each separated by a glockenspiel chiming seven o'clock, once in the evening and again in the morning. These larger divisions correspond to the three sections of a big movement in sonata form: exposition, development, and recapitulation. The deviations from a textbook sonata movement all stem from the programmatic overlay that Strauss impresses on the larger structure. Since there are three characters, there are three main themes, or groups of themes. Strauss himself is by turns jolly, dreamy, and passionate. The very opening motive of three notes recurs constantly and couldn't be simpler. It opens the symphony on the lower strings and bassoons, followed immediately by the "dreamy" melody on the oboe.

Pauline Strauss, announced on the violins, is alternately vivacious, gracious, and somewhat shrewish and quarrelsome considering those jagged rhythms and dissonant harmonies. Her "money phrase" appears, unsurprisingly, on the solo violin very sweetly, before she starts giving orders. Strauss was nothing if not honest, and it was for that very reason that his wife loathed (and maybe feared) his musical family portraits. Baby Franz gets a simple, tranquil melody on the oboe d'amore. It's arguably the most memorable tune in the entire work, but it appears only after a healthy bout of loud "Wha! Wha!" crying in the full orchestra. You can't miss either the wailing or the actual theme, which grows in importance as the work proceeds.

The music bounces along as relatives arrive to see the baby. "So like papa!" Strauss writes over the trumpets, and "So like mama!" over the trombones, just before the end of this initial presentation of themes. The music then proceeds to a delectable Scherzo ("joke" in Italian, but typically a quick movement in dance rhythm) depicting the hustle and bustle of a typical day. Pay particular attention to the accompaniment figure containing one longer and four shorter repeated notes. It becomes a very important motive in the Adagio. The scherzo varies all of the main material, gradually becoming more tranquil until a lusty scream from the baby brings his parents running. They sing a gentle lullaby together—two clarinets—and put the baby to sleep as the clock strikes seven.

The Adagio that passes for the development contains three distinct sections. First, the composer goes to his study to work. As inspiration builds, Strauss develops the "dreamy" oboe tune into a full-fledged romantic melody that builds to a grand climax on the full orchestra featuring the scherzo's repeated-note motive. Then Strauss heads off to bed to make love to his wife. The music turns chromatic and appropriately slithery as Pauline's themes mingle with her husband's, rising in tension to a graphically orgasmic climax with screaming violins and dissonant brass blasting out the repeated-note figure. Strauss would return to this music in his opera *Elektra*, both where the title character sings of her desire for vengeance in her opening monologue and at the peak of the quasi-sexual frenzy in which she dances herself to death at the very end. It's shockingly realistic and intense in either the operatic or symphonic context.

The Adagio's final episode after the sex scene is a wonderfully scored depiction of a dreamy sleep, with memories of all of the main themes and motives fluttering by in delicate, seemingly random procession. Baby Franz returns here for the first time since the Scherzo; he obviously played no part in the prior two sections of the Adagio. As the music gently subsides, the glockenspiel chimes seven once again. Franz wakes up with his characteristic cry, rousing the entire family and initiating the finale.

This is a genuine recapitulation of the work's opening introduction and scherzo, only now the introduction is a double fugue and the scherzo is, well, still a scherzo, depicting "joyful confusion" according to Strauss. The original introduction presented the three main themes in sequence. A fugue does it in combination and has the character of a discussion or, in this case, a robust argument between mama and papa, with baby Franz making his presence felt now and then. The themes of a fugue are called "subjects," and their presentation is called, not too surprisingly, an "exposition." Sections where the subjects are absent are "episodes." A double fugue, as the name implies, means two subjects or themes (papa and mama, with episodes featuring baby), but the genius of Strauss' approach is not just that he recapitulates the opening ideas, but that he does it with a form that is both compressed and programmatically apt.

As for the rest of the finale, despite Strauss' description of it as "joyful confusion," it is really another one of those moments where the story has ended and Strauss takes some time to write abstract, or "absolute," music. It's a vigorous romp based on the main themes and their variations. Notice especially, a couple of minutes before the end, the wild section for horns that consists entirely of a speeded-up version ("diminished," in musical terminology) of the baby's theme. The work concludes brilliantly with the three notes of papa's theme, one of Strauss' very few loud endings.

The *Symphonia Domestica* was premiered at Carnegie Hall in New York. It was a great popular success, so much so that Wanamaker's department store organized subsequent performances on its sales floor, for which Strauss was paid handsomely. This is not as crazy as it sounds today. Department stores catered primarily to a wealthy, cultured, mostly female clientele. They supported musical attractions as part of their marketing programs. Wanamaker's stores in New York and Philadelphia had recital halls or courtyards fitted with pipe organs that provided shoppers with regularly scheduled entertainment. The organ in the Philadelphia Wanamaker's store, now a Macy's, is a historic landmark and one of the largest instruments in the world. It still offers recitals almost daily.

Be that as it may, snobbish critics both in American and Europe, already disgusted with the music's programmatic concept, took the additional performances at Wanamaker's as a sign of Strauss' inartistic materialism. He replied to the effect that there could be nothing wrong with a man making money to support his family. Nevertheless, it was not the tone poem's popular success but the subsequent critical disdain with which posterity has chosen to brand the piece. This is a pity. Strauss was pleased with his effort, and for good reason. From a purely formal point of view, the *Domestica* is one of his most successful orchestral works, and this is because it has a program perfectly suited to the treatment it receives. You don't get one without the other.

Tone Poems II
Places and Things

Nature and Nietzsche: *Aus Italien, Also sprach Zarathustra*, and *An Alpine Symphony*

Aus Italien (From Italy) (1886)
Scoring: piccolo, 2 flutes, 2 oboes, English horn, 2 clarinets, 2 bassoons, contrabassoon, 4 horns, 2 trumpets, 3 trombones, triangle, cymbals, tambourine, snare drum, timpani, harp, strings

It is difficult to understand today just how much consternation Strauss' warmhearted and wholly lovely *Aus Italien* caused when it first appeared. In any other country it might have been called a symphony, such as Berlioz's *Harold in Italy* or Tchaikovsky's *Manfred*. However, with two slowish movements and the sonata-form "first movement" actually placed second, that was impossible in 1880s Germany. To be sure, programmatic German symphonies existed—Joachim Raff (1822–1882), for instance, wrote a whole slew of them, some of them quite popular. So did Ludwig Spohr (1784–1859), a composer of immense reputation during his lifetime whose music had already become dated by the 1880s. But those works, for the most part, took care to follow traditional forms in addition to being programmatic.

Strauss, on the other hand, had already produced two successful traditional symphonies before *Aus Italien* that had been well received by the listening public. Moreover, he had just become the protégé of Brahms champion Hans von Bülow at the Meiningen Court Orchestra. *Aus Italien* marked a decisive turn toward the Wagner/Liszt school of modern composition and, in its way, was a repudiation of Bülow, Liszt's son-in-law, whose wife Cosima had abandoned him for Wagner (thus precipitating to some degree his turn to Brahms). It was a very tangled situation, then, not just aesthetically but politically and personally for Strauss and his circle of friends and acquaintances. Strauss' home base of Munich also remained a conservative backwater, despite the town's temporary and unwilling accommodation of Wagner at the behest of its mad king Ludwig II. Certainly Strauss' own father belonged staunchly to the old guard.

The four movements of *Aus Italien* consist of three landscapes and a concluding, festive, "Neapolitan Folk Life" finale. This last movement quotes the popular tune "Faniculì, Faniculà," which Strauss believed to be a folk song. However, far from being "the uncouth vocal utterance of the people," to use comedienne Anna Russell's felicitous phrase, the song in fact had been written only a few years earlier by Luigi Denza (1846–1922), a composer and later professor of voice at the Royal Academy in London, to celebrate the opening of the Mount Vesuvius funicular railway. The funicular in question was destroyed when Vesuvius erupted in 1944, but the song lives on to this day. On learning of the theft of his tune, Denza promptly sued Strauss for royalties (and won), a singular irony in that Strauss throughout his life was a passionate advocate for composers' rights and copyright reform.

For his part, Strauss' reaction on finding out that the melody was not a folk tune ran something along the lines of, "You mean someone actually *wrote* that?" It would be difficult to imagine a more delightful illustration of the difference between Italian and German aesthetic sensibilities. Aside from the quotation of Denza's song, the most radical element of *Aus Italien* occurs in the scoring of the very first note for the harp in its lowest register. The use of the harp, English horn, and extra percussion, if you recall our previous discussion about the German symphonic tradition, confirms the work's "unsymphonic" credentials. It is very interesting to note that these are precisely the instruments that Strauss omits from his second movement, which is in traditional sonata form.

We cannot at this point know for sure just how consciously Strauss was following (or disregarding) convention in his scoring of this movement, subtitled "In the Roman Ruins," because in all other respects it is the most Straussian-sounding of them all. The principal, rising theme in the trumpet, the urgency of the tempo, and above all the suppleness of the rhythm all point to later Strauss. This last point calls for special comment. The meter is 6/4 freely alternating with 3/2. This means that each bar can be counted either "in two" (1 2 3 **4** 5 6) or "in three" (1 2 3 **4** 5 6), an ambiguity Strauss exploits to give the music that loose, fluid, almost slippery rhythmic quality so typical of his mature work.

The two slowish movements, "In the Roman Countryside" and "On the Beach at Sorrento," are both nature portraits featuring the alternation of lyrical melodies enriched by succulent orchestration—harps, trilling woodwinds for birds, and rich harmony. Although "In the Roman Ruins" is also a landscape, it is a dynamic one. All sonata-form movements are about the conflict between their constituent themes, and therefore they are inherently dramatic. A movement about Roman ruins, for example, cannot describe in music the idea of "Roman" or "ruins" particularly well, but it can portray the process—the struggle and strife of ancient times—and thus capture something of the mood and atmosphere that the sight of the ruins instills in the composer, which he then attempts to express to the listener. To the extent the piece is dramatic, it is also "about" people, or at least human feeling, because that is what drama conveys.

Also sprach Zarathustra (Thus Spoke Zarathustra) (1896)

Scoring: 2 piccolos, 3 flutes, 3 oboes, English horn, 3 clarinets, bass clarinet, 3 bassoons, contrabassoon, 6 horns, 4 trumpets, 3 trombones, 2 tubas, bass drum, cymbals, triangle, glockenspiel, bell, timpani, 2 harps, organ, 16 first and 16 second violins, 12 violas, 12 cellos, 8 basses

Aus Italien, then, consists of two movements illustrating nature, and two representing the human element. In this early work Strauss keeps these concepts separate and distinct, but in his two later tone poems, *Also sprach Zarathustra* and *An Alpine Symphony*, the conflict between humanity and nature constitutes the principal subject of the musical program. Happily, that is just about all you need to know about them in order to understand the extramusical element. Although based on Strauss' reading of German philosopher Friedrich Nietzsche, neither

work attempts to illustrate Nietzschean philosophy, which would have
been pointless since much of it is gibberish and its precise meaning a
subject of controversy even now.

The general appeal of Nietzsche to Strauss lay in his antireligious
views, his description of the impersonal grandeur and mystery of nature
as set against the perpetual striving of humanity, and perhaps most
importantly, his philosophical rejection of Wagner, whose embrace of
Christianity in his last opera (*Parsifal*) and willingness to encourage his
own cult status Nietzsche viewed as selling out to the lowest form of
German bourgeois religiosity. Nevertheless, Strauss actually conceived
of the man-versus-nature program of *Also sprach Zarathustra* long before
he decided what to call the work or even thought about it in Nietzschean
terms at all. He spent a good bit of time considering a range of literary
models, including Goethe's *Faust*, before making his final choice.

In other words, the basic idea behind the work has little uniquely
to do with Nietzsche. The "striving humanity against impassive nature"
theme is as old as civilization, and one ripe with possibilities for musical
exploitation. The ultimate selection of Nietzsche's *Zarathustra* as his
subject did, however, come with one clear advantage beyond Strauss'
own sympathies with the philosopher's views. Like Wagner's favorite
philosopher, Schopenhauer, Nietzsche was musical, with very strong
views on the meaning and value of music as an expression of human
consciousness. He even tried his hand, not very successfully, at composition, and some discs of his works have been recorded. *Zarathustra*,
in particular, in addition to featuring plenty of nature philosophy, contains lots of singing and dancing, with whole sections ("Dance Song,"
"Midnight Song," "Dirge") conceived in musical terms. This permitted
Strauss to organize the work programmatically along purely musical
lines that were still consistent with Nietzsche's book.

Strauss was very happy with the form that he devised for *Also sprach
Zarathustra*, and with good reason. Its thirty-plus continuous minutes
are ingeniously assembled from a handful of distinctive motives whose
emotional significance is easy to grasp, making the musical argument
simple and satisfying to follow—ironic for a piece supposedly concerned
with "philosophy." Indeed, because it does not describe specific events
(with one major exception that we will discuss shortly), the expressive

point of the music is exceptionally clear and free of extramusical complications.

This is also Strauss' most Wagnerian work, in that its organizing principle is not so much the development of longer themes, but rather the interplay of brief, instantly recognizable motives—*Leitmotivs*, in Wagnerian parlance. Strauss surely was aware of what this meant and intended it as a special provocation that his musical colleagues would have understood. Using Wagner's techniques to non-Wagnerian ends was an important aspect of his quest to lead German music in new directions, and he went on to repeat this process similarly in the opera that cemented his reputation as the chief representative of the next phase in the evolution of German music for the stage: *Salome*.

In case you're curious, Zarathustra (Zoroaster) was the founder of the ancient religion of Zoroastrianism, which still exists among a small circle of adherents centered in modern Iran. It was influential as a precursor to the major monotheistic religions, starting with Judaism, and was largely eclipsed by the rise of Islam, but its roots go back many centuries before Christ—exactly how many no one knows for sure. Nietzsche probably chose the name because of the ancient religion's emphasis on the idea that the divine principle is sustained through man's exercise of free will to choose good over evil, but there is absolutely nothing that you need to know about this in listening to Strauss' music, nor do the main ideas espoused by Nietzsche's Zarathustra—the coming of the Superman, the idea of "eternal recurrence," or the famous dictum that "God is dead"—figure in Strauss' program in any meaningful way. Strauss said he conceived the music "freely after Nietzsche," and as already suggested by the compositional history of the work, he wasn't kidding.

The key to listening to Strauss' tone poem rests in knowing where its various sections start and finish, as this is not always obvious and does not necessarily correspond to what their various titles may suggest to you. I used to think that the luscious string theme right after the introduction represented the "Great Longing," but it doesn't. It belongs to the previous section. It's still a great tune, but it is nice to know what it actually represents. This is easy now: most compact discs have index points following the sectional divisions that Strauss indicated in the score, but in the early days of vinyl LPs (never mind in concert) it could be a challenge. The nine sections are:

1. Introduction [sunrise; "Nature" motive]
2. Of Those in the Back-World ["Striving" motive; humankind] (1)
3. Of the Great Longing [transition] (6)
4. Of Joys and Passions [ending in "Digust" motive] (2)
5. The Grave Song [transition] (4)
6. Of Science [fugue on "Nature" motive] (7)
7. The Convalescent [development] (5)
8. The Dance Song [ending in "Disgust" motive] (3)
9. The Night Wanderer's Song [midnight bell; coda—man and nature] (8)

After each section I place a number that indicates its order in the original book, which actually contains dozens of mostly brief sections. As you can see, Strauss has made his selection to create ideal musical continuity, and not to follow the progression found in Nietzsche's collection of Zarathustra's "sayings."

Three principal motives, just listed, bind these various episodes together. The first is the "sunrise" motive of three rising notes on the trumpet that opens the work, made famous from its use in the movie *2001: A Space Odyssey.* This motive also stands for "Nature." Its use in the film was appropriate, since it is about as close to that mysterious black monolith in its simple, unchanging shape as music can get. The next motive occurs at the start of the following section, "Of Those in the Back-World," played low down and softly in the bassoons. It has four notes and also rises, as if groping toward the light. Call it "Striving." The final motive represents negation, or "Disgust" in Nietzsche's words, and it appears loudly in the trombones and tubas at the very end of the section "Of Joys and Passions."

The first two sections present the work's two protagonists, Nature, in the form of that brilliant sunrise, and humankind, the soft "striving" motive followed by a gorgeously lyrical, vocal hymn in the strings gently backed by organ to give the sonority a luminous glow. This tune ends with a gentle new idea that reappears at the end of the love scene in *Ein Heldenleben.* Exactly what significance, if any, it held for Strauss is anyone's guess.

"Of the Great Longing" is a transitional section. Bits of the lyrical tune alternate with the Nature and Striving motives, and the latter evolves into a thrusting gesture on the lower strings, quickly flowing into the next section, the turbulent "Of Joys and Passions." This theme is one of those classic Strauss tunes for strings and horns that packs a lot of notes in a very tricky rhythm into each bar, and this gives it that fluid, propulsive quality so characteristic of his melodies in quick tempos. As already noted, this section ends with the "Disgust" motive growling in the low brass. The texture gradually disintegrates, leading into "The Grave Song," another transitional passage only a couple of minutes long, very similar in its fragmented construction to the previous "Of the Great Longing." The suggestion, clearly, is that all human striving is futile, culminating in death.

Having exhausted the emotional approach in "Of Joys and Passions," Strauss now explores the purely intellectual in a slow, glum, expressively impassive fugue scored mostly for heavily divided strings. This slowly creeps upward from its beginnings in the cellos and basses, leading to its exact opposite: a lyrical transformation of the Striving motive high in the violins, introducing the woodwinds' brief anticipation of "The Dance Song," cut off by the Nature and Disgust motives. A quick crescendo, and the work's most complex and curious section, "The Convalescent," begins with a fast and loud development of the "science" fugue in the brass.

I mentioned previously that there was only one exception to the rule that none of the episodes in this work were explicitly programmatic in the sense that they referred specifically to the action, such as it is, in Nietzsche's book. Well, "The Convalescent" is that exception. In the book, Zarathustra is living in a cave with his buddies, the forest critters. Suddenly, he jumps up shrieking, "Disgust!" and freaks out, before collapsing. "The Convalescent" has two parts separated by a long pause, conveniently dividing the tone poem into two halves. The first part, which works itself into a frenzy culminating in a terrifying return of the Nature motive, perfectly illustrates Zarathustra's hysterical fit. Remember that *development* generally means "human action" of some kind, and this episode is the most developmental in the entire work.

Strauss will employ a similar technique at the start of *Don Quixote* to represent the knight's descent into madness.

After his fit, Zarathustra lapses into a coma that lasts seven days. Music has difficulty portraying a seven-day-long coma, and you probably wouldn't enjoy it even if it could, so Strauss thankfully does not try. Rather, Zarathustra's coma kicks the music back to square one, the evocation of primitive man (the Back-Worlders), before developing into another frantic passage of rushing strings, now based on the Striving motive. This rises through the orchestra, introducing a remarkable passage for chirping flutes, piercing trumpet, and gurgling woodwinds. In the book, what is happening is that Zarathustra has a conversation with his animal friends, who tell him to get out of his cave and experience the world, the "garden of life," and listen in particular to the song of the birds. It is this "sounds of nature" passage that Strauss captures so evocatively.

The animals promise Zarathustra that he will learn to sing new songs, and as the excitement increases the music of the next section, "The Dance Song," starts to take shape—in Strauss, not in Nietzsche, who follows up "The Convalescent" with "Of the Great Longing," for some reason. Strauss' order makes far greater sense. A crash on the cymbal clears the way for the new section to begin. Throughout the work, Strauss has portrayed Man and Nature not just with their own motives, but with individual key areas as well: C major for Nature, and B major/minor for Man. Although next to each other on the scale, the keys outlined by these notes are in fact about as far apart as you can get, and this distance represents their mutual incompatibility. "The Dance Song" attempts a resolution with a melody for solo violin accompanied by oboe with a seven-note figure consisting of the Nature motive (three notes) followed by the Striving motive (four notes).

The tune itself displays at first a folksy, hurdy-gurdy style, which Zarathustra mentions specifically in his chat with the animals. Formally, this episode acts as an exhilarating recapitulation of all of the various motives. Dramatically, the union of Man and Nature gets undermined by the increasing prominence of the Striving motive, reaching a huge and athletic climax that collapses with the twelvefold tolling of the midnight bell, interspersed with the Disgust motive. Thus begins the final

"Song of the Night Wanderer." Strauss' score contains a misprint here. It says "*Nachwandlerlied*" rather than Nietzsche's "*Nachtwandlerlied*," which, thanks to the German language's delicious ability to form long new words by stitching together shorter ones, means something like "Song of Those Who Wander Afterwards" (*nach* = after, *Nacht* = night). This makes no sense at all, which hasn't stopped some sources from insisting on it anyway. The actual text of this song was set by Mahler as the fourth movement of his Third Symphony.

This final climax, however, is not especially tragic, and the final section, which acts as a coda, is gently nostalgic. As the texture becomes ever more diaphanous, the two keys, C major and B major, take over the bottom and top of the orchestra, respectively, and end the work softly but mysteriously, without resolution. Ethereal chords high in the flutes and violins alternate with the Nature motive in pizzicato basses. This is not one of those codas where Strauss feels the need to continue on past the logical point of conclusion, either musically or programmatically. Despite its lack of finality, the ending arrives punctually, without a single wasted note, sounding at once inevitable but oddly unsatisfying, just as Strauss intended.

An Alpine Symphony (1915)

Scoring: 2 piccolos, 4 flutes, 3 oboes, English horn, heckelphone, 4 clarinets, bass clarinet, 4 bassoons, contrabassoon, 8 horns, 4 tenor tubas, 4 trumpets, 4 trombones, 2 tubas, wind machine, thunder sheet, bass drum, cymbals, tam-tam, triangle, snare drum, glockenspiel, cowbells, 2 sets of timpani, 2 harps, organ, celesta, "at least" 18 first and 16 second violins, 12 violas, 10 cellos, 8 basses

Offstage: 12 horns, 2 trumpets, 2 trombones, with 2 flutes, oboes, and 2 clarinets optionally doubled where indicated

Also sprach Zarathustra's unresolved ending turns out to be doubly apt when we consider that it was not Strauss' last word on the subject of man and nature. That honor goes to *An Alpine Symphony*. Once again inspired by Nietzsche, his *Antichrist* this time—as well as a whole host of other influences, including the sudden death of Gustav Mahler in 1911—Strauss' last avowed tone poem has had some rough press.

Sneeringly referred to as "A Day in the Life of an Alp," or "A Film Score in Need of a Film," *An Alpine Symphony*'s reputation has been rehabilitated in recent times owing largely to the opportunity that recordings have offered music lovers to actually hear it in decent sound. What they have discovered has turned out to be, as often as not, very pleasing.

Glamorously scored for a recklessly huge orchestra, the work is indeed cinematic, but that isn't necessarily a bad thing. Unlike *Zarathustra*, which Strauss recalls from time to time at some of the work's climaxes, much of the music in *An Alpine Symphony* is straightforwardly descriptive, even naively so. For example, when Mahler uses cowbells in his Sixth and Seventh Symphonies, the intent is metaphysical and poetic—as a last glimpse of earthly life heard from far away. Strauss, on the other hand, uses cowbells to represent . . . cows. Similarly, Strauss' mother of all Alpine storms, despite being the work's development section (and a very strict one too in terms of thematic workmanship), and notwithstanding its clever placement *after* the formal moment of recapitulation, remains just a storm, part of a long tradition of orchestral storms going back to the baroque period. Even Vivaldi's *The Four Seasons* has one.

Neither *Zarathustra* nor *An Alpine Symphony* has much room for the erotic element that Strauss portrays so well, and that slithery chromatic harmony that often comes with it, although the former work's "Of Joys and Passions" comes close. The Nature motive in *Zarathustra* is built out of the simplest musical intervals, and so is much of the melodic material of *An Alpine Symphony*. Although it requires vast instrumental resources, its textures are simpler, clearer, and less busy than one often finds in Strauss' orchestral writing. Mountains, like pyramids, often take the form of simple geometric shapes, and so do many of Strauss' themes, the musical analogue to geometry in this case being a reliance on consonant harmony and diatonic melody (which means tunes that remain rooted in their fundamental key).

As a result of these compositional decisions, *An Alpine Symphony* has an "old-fashioned" feel to it, even with its advanced orchestration and irrespective of the undeniably appropriate treatment of its subject matter. Fans of the radical Strauss in works such as *Salome* and *Elektra*, never mind the earlier tone poems including *Zarathustra*, can very easily see the piece as regressive. But in terms of Strauss' compositional development it is an important work, because it signals a move toward an increasingly simplicity and directness of expression that became a permanent feature of his art after World War I. Although never a neo-classicist in the sense that, say, Stravinsky or Hindemith was, Strauss evolved strikingly in that direction. The difference is that the younger composers evoked earlier musical forms and idioms in a self-consciously stylized way. It was an aspect of their modernity, and of their often acerbic, biting antiromanticism.

Strauss, on the other hand, lived and breathed the German classical tradition. He was raised in it, and it formed a natural and significant aspect of his compositional makeup. It was not incompatible with his essentially romantic orientation, but part of a single musical continuum in which he was merely the latest representative. To his colleagues, however, his decision to embrace his classical roots, especially with regard to harmony, only made him seem increasingly out of touch with more recent developments.

All of these considerations come into play with respect to *An Alpine Symphony*, but few of them have relevance to listeners today in forming a fair appraisal of the work itself. In their way, Strauss' nature portraits are as mundane as his musical depictions of daily life in the *Symphonia Domestica*. He was not concerned with profundity for its own sake. His goal was accuracy of description, and the beauty that results from cloak-ing even the most ordinary things in music of extraordinary technical finish. Mahler, who was nothing if not metaphysical, once remarked that he and Strauss were tunneling from opposite sides of a mountain, destined someday to meet in the middle. In other words, there are many roads to the same goal, and *An Alpine Symphony* represents a particu-larly extreme case of the Straussian path. It clears the air for much of the music to come.

This view of the work tends to contradict the opinion of many other writers, even some who are dedicated Strauss scholars. In their view, Strauss at this point in his career was looking almost exclusively for operatic subjects and had little interest in further tone poems. The lengthy gestation period of the work, more than a decade and a half, tends to support this theory. Nevertheless, Strauss did compose *An*

Alpine Symphony and professed himself pleased with the result, especially its orchestration. The fact that he had other, stronger interests at
the time does not mean that he lavished less care on the piece than he
would have otherwise. Furthermore, the traditional assessment ignores
the work's place in his overall development, and that seems to me a mistake. If *An Alpine Symphony* seems different from Strauss' earlier tone
poems in its musical language, it is because at this point in his career he
was in a different place, not because he had exhausted the possibilities
of the tone poem as a medium for musical expression.

Strauss divided *An Alpine Symphony* into twenty-two sections, rang-
ing in length from just a few seconds ("At the Waterfall" and "The Mist
Rises") to more than six minutes. Not surprisingly, the longest section,
"Ausklang" or "Conclusion," isn't about anything at all, being merely a
nostalgic meditation on the work's main themes. The final part, "Night,"
thus has something of the character of a coda to the coda, but it's only a
couple of minutes in total. You can find the full list of episodes below,
and although it may make the work look fragmentary, the music really
is continuous from start to finish.

1. Night
2. Sunrise
3. The Ascent
4. Entry into the Forest
5. Wandering Beside the Brook
6. At the Waterfall
7. Apparition
8. On Flowering Meadows
9. On the Alpine Pasture
10. Through Thickets and Undergrowth on Mistaken Paths
11. On the Glacier
12. Dangerous Moments
13. On the Summit
14. Vision
15. The Mist Rises
16. The Sun Is Gradually Obscured
17. Elegy

18. Calm Before the Storm
19. Storm and Thunder, Descent
20. Sunset
21. Conclusion (of the Journey)
22. Night

As these titles suggest, the various parts contain music of widely varying character. The motive of the mountain, heard in the low brass at the very start, is suitably massive and imposing, while the ensuing "Sunrise," if not quite as glorious as that in *Also sprach Zarathustra*, is pretty impressive in its own right. Besides, Strauss has saved the work's most *Zarathustra*-like moment for the brass-laden climax of "On the Summit." The music representing the climb itself, a metaphor for human striving and noble endeavor, consists of four principal themes. Two of them appear during "The Ascent": a striding melody in the strings, ending with a leaping brass fanfare leading to a hunting episode (not indicated as such) for tons of offstage horns, trumpets, and trombones.

"Entry into the Forest," signaled by a crash on the tam-tam that's curiously difficult to hear in most performances, introduces a darker tune on the brass, while the final symbol of the journey, a lovely, lyrical string theme that Strauss admitted likely came from the finale of Max Bruch's First Violin Concerto, first appears at the end of "Apparition." This last is one of four longer, developmental sections that suggest a kind of commentary or reflection on the journey to that point. The others are "Vision," "Elegy," and "Conclusion," while the titles of the remaining episodes speak for themselves. You will notice that wherever Strauss suggests the journey's progress, the main theme of "The Ascent" is present somewhere, often in the bass, like a strong but unobtrusive current pushing the music forward.

Finally, the storm sequence both develops the previous themes in dynamic combination and accomplishes a very speedy descent by recalling them in intensified and extremely condensed form. Notice, for example, how the reprise of "At the Waterfall" recalls that particular stage of the journey and at the same time represents the downpour of rain during the storm. It works both ways. At the climax of the storm,

Strauss asks for a "thunder machine," an effect seldom realized with the necessary cataclysmic volume either in concert or on recordings. The modern "thunder sheet," a thin metal contraption hung at the back of the orchestra and wiggled at the appropriate moment, hardly does the music justice.

When the sun comes out after the storm's conclusion, Strauss features the organ, just as he did in *Zarathustra*. The organ, with its inexpressive, nonvocal timbre, perfectly represents the impassivity of nature, just as it has served for centuries to emphasize the spiritual or nonhuman in religious music. Strauss, of course, was fully aware of the organ's traditional purpose, and it is no accident that he chooses to write what is effectively religious music in the most purely secular context possible. At the very end, all that remains is night, and the mountain, just as at the start. The entire journey has taken about half a day, sunup to sunset, and Strauss' musical travelogue condenses it all into approximately forty-five to fifty minutes.

Death, With and Without Transfiguration: *Tod und Verklärung* and *Metamorphosen*

Tod und Verklärung (Death and Transfiguration) (1889)
Scoring: *3 flutes, 2 oboes, English horn, 2 clarinets, bass clarinet, 2 bassoons, contrabassoon, 4 horns, 3 trumpets, 3 trombones, tuba, timpani, tam-tam, 2 harps, strings*

Death and Transfiguration was composed in the first flush of Strauss' conversion to the Wagnerian cause, and it features his most philosophically Wagnerian program. An artist lies dying, and the music suggests his faltering heartbeat, a rhythm that will recur throughout the work. The passionate music of the Allegro sections depicts his striving for unattainable perfection. At times he glimpses it, but he cannot grasp it and find fulfillment. Peaceful interludes depict his youth and moments of happiness, but always his restless quest intervenes. Finally, with a last violent convulsion he dies, and in death his spirit grasps the transcendent culmination that eluded him in life. It's hot stuff, grounded in Wagner's belief in the artist's sacred mission, as well as the romantic notion of fulfillment in death as expressed most tellingly in *Tristan und Isolde*.

Strauss' guide to all things Wagnerian was his friend Alexander Ritter, composer of the tone poem *Kaiser Rudolf's Ride to the Grave* and other jolly bonbons for the most part forgotten today. To celebrate Strauss' achievement, and because all Wagnerians considered themselves literary as well as musical geniuses, he wrote a long-winded poem describing the music. Strauss graciously appended it to the score. Ritter's poem says virtually nothing helpful beyond the description of the work just provided, and it actually can prove deceptive in that the balance of the details in verse does not and cannot correspond to the actual amount of time that Strauss spends depicting the various scenes in music. For example, Ritter dispatches the "transfiguration" business in a single line at the very end, while Strauss spends a good five or six minutes at it, or about a quarter of the length of the entire piece. It's also very unclear, at the end of the day, just what "transfiguration" means—far better just to listen to it.

If you look at the orchestration list, you can see right away that Strauss planned to emphasize the darker, deeper timbres of the orchestra. He omits the piccolo and all high-pitched percussion (triangle, cymbals, glockenspiel). All of the lower members of the woodwind section are represented (English horn, bass clarinet, and contrabassoon), and from the optional percussion section only the tam-tam, which has always been used to represent death and solemnity. It's amazing how big a difference a simple decision such as the omission of the piccolo makes. This smallest member of the flute family can be piercingly loud, and its absence ensures that the turbulent bits retain their dark coloring and that the transfiguration episode is glowing but never screechy.

Strauss himself described the form of *D&T*, as it's often called, as a melody that gradually takes shape only at the very end, and that's just what happens. The introduction contrasts two ideas: death, with its dark colors and broken rhythms, and the recollection of happier times past, featuring woodwind solos over harp arpeggios ("arpeggios" are simply chords with the notes played sequentially rather than simultaneously;

it is something harps do especially well, as you can tell from the name of the instrument, which is *arpa* in Italian, as in "arpeggio").

The Allegro section starts off with a loud thwack on the timpani and groping lower strings. The violent struggle is constantly interrupted by the "heartbeat" rhythm of the introduction on timpani and brass. At the very end of the first Allegro, the rising theme of transfiguration appears for the first time, briefly, in the horns, before subsiding into what is effectively the second subject of a sonata-form exposition: the calm, pastoral melodies on solo woodwinds and strings with harp that sound like peaceful recollections of happier times.

Once again the tempo increases, and the development section begins with woodwind fanfares and a new, aspiring theme in the violins. You hear very clearly how all the previous themes plus the death rhythm combine in a furious struggle leading, at last, to what sounds like the arrival of the "transfiguration" theme, nobly, in the brass. This tune appears three times, each time more grandly, and each time failing to find its climactic resolution. The last attempt sends the music right back to the beginning of the introduction, only much shortened, as is the return of the Allegro. This time, with thudding timpani and brass chords and a rising chromatic scale in the woodwinds (a wonderfully evocative effect suggesting the soul flying upward), the dying artist gives up the ghost and a *mezzo-forte* stroke on the tam-tam—often underplayed in performance—announces his death.

Over steady beats on the tam-tam and tolling bell sounds from the harps, Strauss orchestrates a moment of stillness and quiet anticipation, starting at the bottom of the orchestra and coming to rest on a very high, ethereal note in the violins. Then the coda begins: the theme of transfiguration finally appears as a complete melody, rising in power and majesty in combination with the "happiness" melody of the introduction. This builds to an absolutely blinding climax, before fading away contentedly with closing measures that keep you guessing as to when the end will actually happen and that surprise you with their punctuality and fitness when it finally does.

Death and Transfiguration was for some time Strauss' most popular tone poem, for reasons having nothing to do with the fact that it is a wonderful piece of music. It is one of the more modest of his mature orchestral works in terms of forces required, and its self-evidently "profound" program flattered rather than offended the taste of contemporary audiences. There are no graphic sex scenes, no depictions of anarchic mayhem, and no parodies of religion or bourgeois values. The theme of death is also something of a German specialty; don't ask me why. Gloom and misery seem to come with the territory, but Strauss was not an inherently gloomy composer. Quite the opposite. In fact, it wasn't until the very end of his life that he returned to the theme of death in a tone poem, and it turned out to be one of his last and very greatest works.

Metamorphosen: Study for 23 Solo Strings (1945)
Scoring: 10 violins, 5 violas, 5 cellos, 3 basses

Metamorphosen, subtitled *Study for 23 Solo Strings*, never gets included in the standard list of Strauss tone poems, which is puzzling, because it has long been known that the work has a programmatic basis. The problem is that no one is completely sure what the program is. Various theories have been suggested, from the Goethe poem "No One Will Know Himself," to a lament for the destruction of German musical cultural institutions in World War II, even to a memorial tribute on the death of Hitler (a ridiculous notion). The title may refer variously to Ovid's *Metamorphosis*; Goethe's poem "The Metamorphosis of Plants," or his eponymous scientific study; or perhaps even the work's own formal process, which is a type of evolving variation on two principal ideas. One thing is certain: the coda quotes from the funeral-march second movement of Beethoven's "Eroica" Symphony, over which Strauss has written "In Memoriam!" The work's main theme seems to recall the Beethoven, but Strauss claimed that he was unaware of the resemblance until he came to the end, when the theme "metamorphoses" into a direct citation.

However, the fact that we don't know the program doesn't mean that the work lacks one or is not a tone poem. Paul Sacher (1906–1999) commissioned it for his Basel Chamber Orchestra. We owe Sacher a debt of gratitude for his support of just about every major twentieth-century composer, and some of the best-known contemporary orchestral works were written for him. These include Stravinsky's *Concerto in D*, Frank Martin's *Petite symphonie concertante*, and both Bartók's *Divertimento* and his *Music for Strings, Percussion and Celesta*. Strauss was so moved by *Metamorphosen* that he refused to conduct the premiere, although he assisted at rehearsals.

Strauss' emotionally neutral subtitle *Study for 23 Solo Strings* cannot convey the richness and complexity of the contrapuntal texture that operates throughout *Metamophosen*, or its expressive impact. The volume of sound that Strauss extracts from his limited ensemble is quite amazing, though at first the music can be difficult to follow on account of the relentless polyphony and relatively monochromatic textures. The lack of orchestral color, however, forces the listener to concentrate on the constant thematic metamorphosis that lies at the heart of the work's formal construction.

Interestingly, the music's overall shape is quite similar to that of *Death and Transfiguration*: a slow introduction, a quick central section, and a return to the initial slower tempo. It plays continuously for about twenty-five to twenty-eight minutes in most performances and falls into the above three sections, here of roughly equal length, followed by a shorter coda. First there is the slow introduction, which gradually accelerates into the quick episode, marked "Agitato." This continues to speed up in stages, reaching a climax of exceptional intensity and leading to the loud, unison return to the opening section, now abbreviated in length, and thence to the coda containing, just before the very end, the Beethoven quotation in the lower strings. The music is so fluid, though, that you may very well not notice when one section ends and another begins, and Strauss has covered his tracks so as to make his transitions absolutely seamless.

The unison return to the opening, at least, is fairly obvious. It occurs about two-thirds of the way through. However, don't be fooled by the moment some twenty minutes in where the music stops suddenly, and then resumes *fortissimo*. That moment occurs in the middle of the recapitulation of the opening introduction. Perhaps the most remarkable fact about *Metamorphosen* is that there are very few moments when one of its main ideas is not present, and distinctly audible, and so the key to listening is to know those themes. They appear right at the beginning. Pay special attention to:

1. The first four chords for cellos and basses with which the work begins. Those arresting, unstable harmonies constantly recur and are hard to miss whenever they appear.
2. The "Beethoven" theme. If you know the "Eroica" Symphony, Strauss' idea shares the descending motive (DA-dum, DA-dum, with the accent on the shorter, first note) in the second phrase of Beethoven's tune. This is a very old *topos* in Western music, going back hundreds of years and symbolic of grief or weeping when it occurs, as here, in dark minor keys. The apotheosis of this motive, one that Strauss also knew well, occurs in the "Lacrimosa" from Mozart's Requiem. Strauss' theme always starts with four repeated notes before the weeping motive, and the viola introduces it.
3. The "Beethoven" theme, version two. This idea, also on the violas, follows immediately and clearly derives from the tune just described, and so really can't be called an independent theme. It starts with the same four repeated notes as the original version and then features a different descending phrase that does not contain the weeping motive. It then flows on more swiftly with movement in triplets (three notes played in two beats). This idea, minus the four repeated notes, becomes the source of much of the contrasting music in major, sunnier keys.

As this description suggests, the music begins evolving right from the start and continues to do so until the very end, but there is also a great deal of straight repetition so that the metamorphosis of the themes always occurs in close proximity to one of them in its original form. The result is almost ritualistic in feeling, a ceremonial act of mourning where the emotion of grief continually breaks through and distorts the original rigid melodic shapes. That makes the music very intense. It's the kind of work that only a very experienced composer could have written, since it requires a very delicate sense of timing and feeling for form.

Whatever inspiration lies behind *Metamorphosen*, it makes a fitting and beautiful, if terribly sad, conclusion to the series of tone poems that began six decades earlier with the youthful and sunny *Aus Italien*.

Part 2

Theatrical and Vocal Music (Operas, Ballets, Suites, and Songs)

Strauss and the German Operatic Tradition

trauss' operas are as important historically as Wagner's, if for different reasons. Before Wagner, there were many German operas, but aside from Mozart's *The Abduction from the Seraglio* (*Die Entführung aus dem Serail*) and *The Magic Flute* (*Die Zauberflöte*), Weber's *Der Freischütz*, and Beethoven's *Fidelio*, practically none held the international stage, and the Beethoven was still something of an acquired taste (actually, it still is). Wagner, of course, was a very great composer, but until the 1890s his mature operas—from *Lohengrin* on—were seldom produced, and his reputation rested as much on orchestral excerpts and on his writings as on actual performances. What is more, colossal as they are, Wagner produced only seven major works: *The Flying Dutchman*, *Tannhäuser*, *Lohengrin*, the four *Ring* operas (which count as one), *Tristan und Isolde*, *Die Meistersinger*, and *Parsifal*.

In the 1890s and early 1900s, it was by no means clear just how exportable Wagner's works would turn out to be. Although he never articulated a theory of opera in the same way that Wagner did, both Strauss' words and deeds reveal his understanding of the need to broaden the range of German opera in order to keep it at the forefront of modern music. Since Wagner's death, exactly one German work had shown the potential to enter the international repertoire: Engelbert Humperdinck's *Hänsel und Gretel*, which received its premiere under Strauss in 1893. Humperdinck turned out to be a one-shot wonder. Nothing else of his achieved anything like similar acclaim, and *Hänsel* was in any case a charming if obvious tribute to Wagner in both orchestral technique and melodic content. The fact that Humperdinck was unable to follow up on his success, despite writing further "fairy-tale" operas virtually identical in style, proved that his chosen path was destined to become an aesthetic dead end.

You may well ask at this point, "What was so special about Wagner? Why was he so important?" The fact is, there were lots of German opera composers in the nineteenth century, including popular names like Lortzing, Marschner, and Nicolai, who wrote some excellent pieces rooted in the prevailing Italian style. For just that reason, their operas remained strictly for local consumption. They were German composers, but their operas were basically German in language only. A truly national style of operatic composition demanded a fusion of something originally German—the symphonic style of Haydn, Mozart, and Beethoven—with the historical conventions of the operatic stage. That meant Wagner. Weber had been heading in Wagner's direction in the early nineteenth century, but his untimely death in 1826, aged only thirty-nine, left the field open until Wagner showed up to take the process to its logical conclusion.

Wagner was a radical. His music was of a sophistication and modernity that advanced the aesthetics not just of German opera, but of Western music generally. However, establishing German opera as a unique, living institution with a style at once national and universal, capable of standing alongside the Italian and French schools, required a young composer of Wagnerian daring willing to take the next step in ratifying what the older man had achieved. There has never been a "school" of just one person. Verdi and Puccini, though recognizably members of the Italian school, did not simply copy the style of Donizetti or Bellini, nor did Donizetti or Bellini slavishly imitate the elder Rossini (who actually outlived them both).

The challenge for Strauss as an operatic composer, as he soon discovered, was heightened by the existence of the cult led by Wagner's wife Cosima. Strauss was on friendly terms with the Wagnerites, at least initially, and understood the need to treat the family very diplomatically. They were, after all, German musical royalty and he was a horn player's kid from Munich just starting out on his career as a conductor and composer. He needed them more than they needed him. Like most cults, Wagner's rapidly had become conservative, dogmatic, and stultifying. Its followers saw him as the culmination of German musical development, as an endpoint, when in fact he actually represented the beginning, the potential founder of a new school of German opera. They could not admit what Strauss, trained as he had been by his father to revere the classics, never forgot: that German art was bigger than Wagner, and however great he was, it had to get over him in order to move forward and retain its vital force.

From a purely musical point of view, Wagner's Leitmotiv technique and symphonic construction had to form the basis of the new German style. That was just common sense, and Strauss embraced this direction from the start, regarding his symphonic poems as studies for the operas to come. Where Strauss broke with Wagner was in his choice of subjects, his philosophy, and his vision of operatic dramaturgy. Wagner may have cloaked his work in nationalistic rhetoric, but his roots lay in French grand opera, and he reveled in its slow-moving, epic style. Strauss' principal models were Mozart and Gluck (more on this shortly). The impact they had on his operas was profound, and it allowed him to adapt Wagnerian stylistics to resoundingly non-Wagnerian plotlines. In this he may have found some support from his favorite philosopher, Friedrich Nietzsche, whose condemnation of Wagner offered a helpful alternative aesthetic in a highly unlikely form: Bizet's *Carmen*.

Premiered in 1875, George Bizet's *Carmen* is about as antithetical to Wagnerian philosophy and aesthetics as it is possible to be. Wagner's characters are mostly mythological figures, or gods and goddesses. Carmen is a gypsy worker in a cigarette factory. The characters in Bizet's opera are all lower-class, contemporary, and realistic. Wagner's women, for the most part, are larger-than-life symbols of feminine virtue. Carmen shamelessly flaunts her sexuality, revels in it, and uses it to her advantage. Her insistence on preserving her own personal freedom leads to her death. However, the most strikingly non-Wagnerian feature of *Carmen* is that the main character is—Carmen.

It is a peculiarity of Wagner's art that none of his operas focus primarily on strong female characters. The only ones whose titles feature a female lead are *Tristan und Isolde*, where Isolde gets second billing to Tristan, and *Die Walküre*, one of the four *Ring* operas. Strauss composed fifteen operas, and nine of them are titled explicitly after the female lead, while three others, *Der Rosenkavalier*, *Intermezzo*, and *Capriccio*, might as well have been since women take the main roles.

Wagner's strongest female character, Brünnhilde, is the daughter of the god Wotan. In *Die Walküre*, her father condemns her to live as a mortal woman, and she gets a very wimpy new Leitmotiv as a result, one of Wagner's worst. Strauss' Empress in *Die Frau ohne Schatten* is also the daughter of a godlike figure, Keikobad, ruler of the spirit realm. At the end of the opera, her father *rewards* her by turning her into a mortal woman. Strauss' closest approach to a character like Carmen is undoubtedly Salome, his first great soprano role. The Judean princess might be kinkier and more disturbed than Bizet's gypsy, but the two share a sexual frankness and lack of inhibition that shocked contemporary audiences to their core.

Wagner's lead characters are, for the most part, tenors. Strauss disliked the tenor voice, probably finding it too Italian. His protagonists are sopranos, and his male leads tend to be baritones. Wagner's operas are long—often very long. Strauss certainly could write long too, and sometimes did, but almost never as long as Wagner, and many of his best operas have only a single act and last less than two swiftly paced hours. Wagner, for the most part, wrote tragedies, and the humor in his single mature comedy, *Die Meistersinger*, seldom strikes listeners as especially funny. Strauss lavished much of his operatic talent in later life on comedies, and for this reason he has not been taken as seriously as he deserves to be.

Wagner was a control freak whose grandiosity and megalomania, as well as his pretentions to philosophical depth, point to a fundamental insecurity in his psychological makeup. This is why he insisted on writing his own texts and created the notion of the *Gesamtkunstwerk*, or "Total Artwork," in which the composer controlled all aspects of the production, down the last details of lighting and staging. In such circumstances, you are only as good as your weakest link, and not surprisingly, Wagner's talent was unequally distributed. He was a very great composer, a tolerable poet for musical purposes, and a pretty weak stage director and theatrical producer.

Strauss, on the other hand, was completely comfortable in his own skin. He knew his strengths and weaknesses, and though perfectly capable of writing his own texts, he preferred a stimulating collaboration to working alone. He was the most loyal of partners: to his wife, his children, his friends, his librettists, his publishers, his attorneys, his accountants, and his conductors. When the Nazis attempted to suppress the name of Jewish librettist Stefan Zweig at the 1935 premiere of *Die schweigsame Frau* (The Silent Woman), Strauss insisted that it be reinstated in the program even though it led to the opera's later performances being canceled, and ultimately to his break with the Nazi regime. In short, his personality was not Wagnerian at all, and his operas reflect this.

Just how many of the above factors Strauss exploited consciously in creating post-Wagnerian German opera, and to what extent he simply was following his natural inclinations anyway, remains an open question. He had such a keen sense of his own abilities and was such a shrewd manager of his budding career that it is hard to believe that anything he did lacked conscious planning. What matters is that he succeeded in building on Wagner's advances in orchestral technique in order to take operatic composition in wholly new directions, so much so that Straussian opera became one of the international standards to which younger composers aspired. In his hands, and not Wagner's, German opera became a "school."

Strauss' operas and other theatrical works fall naturally into several groups, rather like the tone poems. There are the operas based on classical Greek history and mythology, the works that celebrate the European culture of the Enlightenment, the domestic comedies, the exotic (and erotic) orientalist works, and then a couple of "outliers," *Guntram* and *Friedenstag*. These are not inviolable distinctions. Opera is inherently heterogeneous, and elements of different categories often mix and mingle, but it is still a useful way to get a handle on the subject and organize the following discussion.

The Greek Operas

Six Heroines: Iphigenia, Elektra, Ariadne, Helen, Daphne, and Danae

In order to understand Strauss' fascination with Greek operatic subjects, we need to start at the beginning. The first operas in the history of Western music appeared around the late 1500s and early 1600s. They were designed with the aim of recapturing the dramatic conventions of classical Greek theater, and they set subjects drawn from Greek mythology. The very first opera to survive in complete form (because a score was published) is Claudio Monteverdi's *L'Orfeo*, subtitled "a fable in music," performed as part of aristocratic wedding celebrations in Mantua in 1607. The opera tells the story of Orpheus and Eurydice: how he travels to Hades to persuade Pluto to release her back to the land of the living and convinces him through the power of music. Pluto agrees, but only on condition that Orpheus not look at her until they reach the mortal realm, but she needles him into turning around for a quick glance, and so he loses her again. Orpheus returns home alone, only to be torn to pieces by the Maenads, followers of the god Dionysus. In an opera planned for a festive wedding, that sad ending wouldn't do, so the librettist, Alessandro Striggio, has Apollo come down out of the sky and invite Orpheus to join him in the heavens, and then everyone dances a celebratory *moresca*.

As you can see from this ending, ultimately there is often a conflict between drama and opera. The story of Orpheus is supposed to end tragically. The word *drama* comes from the ancient Greek word for "action." Most of Striggio's final act consists of Orfeo's lament over his loss of Eurydice for all time, with his death (in the original legend) occurring as a direct result of his renunciation of earthly pleasures and his disillusionment with the gods. In the opera, Striggio's Apollo tells

Orfeo, in effect, "Quit moping around and let's hang out together." Orfeo replies, "Deal," and they exit, taking with them any remaining shred of dramatic tension, leaving the chorus of nymphs and shepherds behind to party without them.

Opera is Italianized Latin. It is the plural of *opus*, or "work," and signifies a mixture of the arts, including singing, dance, acting, and the visual elements of scenic design. Drama moves at the natural pace of human speech and human action and reaction. Opera, especially the comic variety, may have moments that proceed at a similar pace, but as soon as something happens that requires an emotional response, the action stops dead in its tracks so that the various characters can express themselves in song. That is the very antithesis of drama. So is the practical need to adjust the plotline to accommodate the demands of singers, dancers, musicians, and anyone else who happens to be involved and has to be given something striking to do.

Nevertheless, opera is "dramatic," in its way. The degree to which purely musical considerations take precedence over the dramatic at any given time constitutes the history of the form. At its most basic, this conflict can be seen as a tension between text and music. Which is more important: what the words say, or the elaboration of the music that gives them expressive depth? Over the past four centuries, a certain cyclical pattern has become established wherein musical priorities encroach on the dramatic, gradually crowding them out and replacing them with rigid formal conventions in which the text serves as a sort of scaffolding supporting a standardized musical superstructure. Then a reformer appears who sweeps away the current paradigm, usually under the guise of a return to natural human expression in which text and music coexist in a more harmonious equilibrium.

Strauss/Gluck: *Iphigenie auf Tauris* (1890)

Major Characters: Iphigenie (Iphigenia) (soprano); Orest (Orestes) (baritone); Toas, King of Scythia (baritone); Pylades, Orestes' friend (tenor)

Scoring: piccolo, 2 flutes, 2 oboes, 2 clarinets, 2 bassoons, 2 horns, 2 trumpets, 3 trombones, bass drum, cymbals, triangle, timpani, strings

Strauss was one of the reformers who ushered in a new paradigm. The first of them was Christoph Willibald Gluck (1714–1787), whose so-called reform operas, with a single exception (*Armida*), all avail themselves of classical Greek subjects. Strauss' initial operatic project was not *Guntram*, his first wholly original opera, but rather an updating and arrangement for modern orchestra of Gluck's 1779 opera *Iphigénie en Tauride* (Iphigenia in Tauris). In making his arrangement, he was following in the footsteps of two illustrious predecessors, Wagner and Berlioz, both of whom recast Gluck scores for the modern stage. In considering Strauss' "Greek" operas, then, it helps to understand his relationship to Gluck and to the operatic revolution that he inherited and continued.

Of the composers who qualify as operatic reformers, including Gluck, Wagner, and Strauss, Gluck was by far the most important, because he had the most to do. Opera, where Gluck found it in the early eighteenth century, consisted largely of acres of lightly accompanied sung speech designed to move plot along as quickly as possible ("*secco* [dry] recitative"), followed by arias, or songs, for the singers, almost invariably in the same ABA form, with the return of the "A" section offering the singer the opportunity to embellish the vocal line with a mass of improvised ornaments or decorations, according to the artist's taste (or lack thereof). The same librettos were used over and over by different composers, who seldom had the right to choose the subject. Everything was designed to show off the virtuosity of the singers, the dancers (especially in France), and the wizardry of the set designers.

For his first "reform" opera, in an obvious homage to Monteverdi, Gluck chose the legend of Orpheus, reduced to its bare essentials. There are only three characters, Orpheus, Eurydice, and Cupid, plus the chorus. The opera omits the scene of Eurydice's death. When it starts, Orpheus is already in mourning. The dances are incorporated fluidly into the action, and the music plays continuously, with no "dry" recitative. This means that much of it must move at or close to the pace of speech with full orchestral accompaniment, reflecting the sense of the words. The vocal line is stripped of unnecessary ornaments, and the result is lean, exciting, and passionate. Gluck later codified his reforms in the written preface to his opera *Alceste*, a thrilling work whose gripping, single-minded intensity prefigures Strauss' *Elektra*.

The Gluck opera that Strauss worked on, *Iphigénie en Tauride*, takes these reforms even further. Its most famous number, "Oh, Unhappy Iphigenia," is based on an earlier piece that literally made Gluck famous all over Europe. In its original form it was a not-quite-typical baroque ABA "da capo" ("repeat from the beginning") aria. What made it atypical is the fact that its principal theme has no internal repetitions at all, being a continuously unfolding melody from start to finish. The version in *Iphigénie* strips out the "B" section, cuts the repeat, and allows this haunting and pathetic tune to continue until, at its climax, Iphigenia is joined by the female chorus, and the music flows onward into the next scene. The result: a staggeringly beautiful, natural expression of human feeling effortlessly integrated into the ongoing action of the larger drama.

It is important to understand in this context that "natural expression" does not refer to the plotline or the situation. Gluck's operas remain full of gods and goddesses, mythological characters, magic potions, improbable situations, and other fantastic elements. What is "natural," or real, is that the reaction of the characters and the feelings they express must arise believably from the situation, however weird or silly it may seem. There should be no pointless interruptions by superfluous characters, meaningless plot entanglements, unexplained and unmotivated changes of face, and similar incongruities. For example, Gluck's *Orpheus and Eurydice* also ends happily: Eurydice comes back to life, but only after the gods take pity on Orpheus when he sings the most moving and beautiful aria in the entire work, "Che farò senza Euridice?" ("What Shall I Do Without Eurydice?"). That aria has a dramatic purpose. It also became one of the greatest hits of the 1760s.

After Gluck, and later Mozart, Wagner's reforms were narrower in scope and limited mainly to enrichment of the orchestral accompaniments at the expense of the vocal line, and to humanizing the mechanics of French grand opera, in which the traditional love story risked being drowned in a sea of historical pageantry and special scenic effects. Wagner regarded himself as the culmination of the process initiated by Gluck, but then again he regarded himself as the culmination of art generally, so we needn't take that too seriously. As already noted, Strauss' job consisted of reforming Wagner—rejecting Wagnerian philosophical pretensions by choosing subjects in which the relationship between text and music could be reexamined in more human, even bourgeois terms, while preserving Wagner's advances in symphonic construction and musical continuity.

Strauss accomplished this, in part, in the same way that Gluck did: by taking a fresh look at well-known Greek subjects, thereby affirming the universal validity of his compositional style and technique in terms of these timeless characters and their stories. You can see this process at its most basic without hearing a single note. Just have a look at the scoring listed at the beginning of this section. For *Iphigenie auf Tauris*, which is an arrangement, Strauss is almost 100 percent faithful to Gluck's own orchestration.

Elektra (1908)

Major Characters: Elektra (soprano); Chrysothemis, her sister (soprano); Orest (Orestes), their brother (baritone); Klytaemnestra, their mother (alto or mezzo-soprano); Aegisth (Aegisthus), Klytaemnestra's lover (tenor)

Scoring: 2 piccolos, 3 flutes, 2 oboes, English horn, heckelphone (bass oboe), 5 clarinets, 2 basset horns, bass clarinet, 3 bassoons, contrabassoon, 8 horns, 4 Wagner tubas, 6 trumpets, bass trumpet, 3 trombones, bass trombone, tuba, glockenspiel, triangle, tambourine, snare drum, cymbals, castanets, bass drum, rute (bundle of sticks), tam-tam, celesta, 2 harps, 2 sets of timpani, 8 first violins, 8 second violins, 8 third violins, 6 fourth violins, 6 first violas, 6 second violas, 6 third violas, 6 first cellos, 6 second cellos, 8 basses

Compare Gluck's orchestra to the musically original *Elektra*, which is one of two works (the other is *Die Frau ohne Schatten*) containing the largest forces that Strauss ever required. He was limited only by what he reasonably expected would fit in the orchestra pit in the largest opera houses. Even today, performing *Elektra* offers most venues a serious logistical challenge.

Musically speaking, *Elektra* is Strauss' most modern-sounding score, if by this we mean its level of dissonance. Although still a resolutely tonal work, it has moments, especially during the scene between Elektra and Klytaemnestra, that verge on atonality, and the sheer complexity of texture sometimes approaches the limit of what the human ear can comprehend. Nevertheless, *Elektra* qualifies as a "reform opera" almost as much as does Gluck's *Orfeo*, particularly in its compactness and wildly non-Wagnerian rapidity of pacing. There are only four main characters: Elektra; her mother, Klytaemnestra; her sister, Chrysothemis; and her brother, Orest (Orestes). All three women are sopranos (Klytaemnestra is a mezzo-soprano); Orestes is a baritone. The other parts are all minor, mostly servants and such, including the lead tenor Aegisth (Aegisthus), Klytaemnestra's lover, who appears for only a few minutes toward the end, in time to get murdered by Orestes.

As with *Orfeo*, there is an extensive backstory that takes place before the opera begins. Enraged by the sacrifice of their daughter Iphigenia (the same one in Gluck's operas), Klytaemnestra takes Aegisthus as her lover and together they kill her husband, Agamemnon, while he is taking a bath. Elektra vows revenge and is driven out of the palace. She now lives like a wild animal, spurned by all, awaiting the return of her brother, Orestes, who is duty-bound to take revenge on his murderous mother and her lover. For this purpose, Elektra has concealed the very axe used to kill her father.

All of this is explained in Elektra's first monologue, but the truth is that you don't really need to know any of it because the plot, as it happens onstage, is self-explanatory and simplicity itself: Elektra is obsessed by the desire to avenge the murder of her father. Her sister, Chrysothemis, is a nice girl yearning for a normal life. She finds Elektra's obsession incomprehensible. Elektra has an argument with her mother and plays on her fears of retribution, but during their conversation Klytaemnestra receives news that delights her and leaves. Chrysothemis then runs in and declares that Orestes is dead. Elektra tells her that the two of them must avenge their father's death. Chrysothemis, terrified, refuses. Elektra resolves to kill her mother and her lover alone, but to her great surprise Orestes shows up and takes care of it for her. She then dances herself to death in a wild orgy of exultation. The entire work plays continuously in a single act, lasting less than two hours (even less with some traditional cuts).

Of course, this synopsis hardly touches on the psychological depth of characterization that Strauss achieves in his music, but it is precisely because the plot is so simple, and the action so limited until the very end, that he has the time to explore these characters and their relationships in such detail through the music. This is operatic drama. The music never holds up the action, but rather creates it. For all that "nothing happens" in the conventional sense—the work is little more than a monologue followed by a series of dialogues between the principals—*Elektra* is absolutely thrilling, operating at a consistently high level of tension unmatched by virtually any other opera.

The very first notes that you hear, the motive symbolizing the dead Agamemnon, are identical in rhythm and shape to the "insanity" motive in *Salome*, to be discussed later. Elektra is haunted by the death of her father and her need for vengeance, just as Salome is obsessed by her desire to possess John the Baptist sexually. Lust is lust, Strauss seems to tell us, and what kind is merely a technicality. The music of Elektra's vengeance, heard in the brass both in her opening monologue and at her final collapse, recalls the repeated-note music of sexual climax in the *Symphonia Domestica* of a few years earlier. I won't go into the psychological nuances of the plot or the characters further; these you can determine for yourself when listening. The point to keep in mind is that *Elektra* remains very much a study in obsession, with music to match.

As already noted, the orchestra in *Elektra* is immense. The clarinet section alone could populate a small town, and some of the violas have to double on violins, a very unusual request. Strauss once said, half facetiously, that the piece should be conducted "like Mendelssohn's fairy music," and there are indeed many moments of astonishingly light and transparent orchestration. Consider the unforgettably tender episode in the "recognition scene" where Elektra can do little more than repeat Orestes' name, and Strauss captures her affection by asking for a trembling vibrato not just from the strings, but from the woodwinds as well. Nevertheless, the climaxes are simply crushing, and there are few passages in all of music as scary as the "whips and chains" scoring that accompanies Klytaemnestra's entrance, an effect produced by the very imaginative use of a rute (bundle of sticks wacked against the bass drum case). You can hear that evil is on the prowl long before it actually arrives.

I also should point out that the effect of Klytaemnestra's music, and much else besides, is reduced when the character comes onstage looking like an extra from the latest zombie film, as may well happen these days. Although she should appear exhausted and dissipated, the music graphically depicts her *inner* turmoil. This it achieves with gripping precision, as it does for all of these very disturbed people, but they should not look like freaks. Indeed, Strauss and librettist Hugo von Hofmannsthal imagined a relatively graceful, classical setting for the drama, one that contrasts strongly with the music's harshness and expressionistic intensity, and places the manic character of Elektra herself in high relief. The palace of Agamemnon is not a ruin, and staging the opera in a rock quarry, dystopian factory, or sewer tunnel not only looks cheap, it lessens some of the purely musical shock value that Strauss clearly intended.

Structurally, *Elektra* has a lot in common with the tone poems. You might call it a huge, modified sonata form, falling into two halves, rather like what we found in *Also sprach Zarathustra*. After the Introduction, Elektra is onstage and singing throughout, making this perhaps the most exhausting single role in the active repertoire of most dramatic sopranos.

Part One
    a. Introduction (the maidservants in the courtyard)
    b. Elektra's monologue
    c. Scene with Chrysothemis
    d. Scene with Klytaemnestra

Part Two
    a. Scene with Chrysothemis
    b. Scene with Orestes
    c. Murder scene
    d. Coda—Elektra's dance of death

As you can see, each half has three scenes, plus an introduction to part one and a coda to part two, the second half thus being almost a mirror image of the first. Elektra's monologue clearly serves as the work's exposition, both verbally, since it explains what is happening, and musically, in that it presents the main themes and motives. The scenes with Elektra's sister and mother are also pretty obviously developmental in nature; that with Orestes is a gentler interlude, while the murder scene and Elektra's death dance act as a modified recapitulation and coda. It won't do to push these formal analogies too far, but they are valid and give the work a strong feeling of unity.

There is a sense, however, in which *Elektra* is atypical of Strauss' Greek operas. Its characters are all larger-than-life, very much in the romantic tradition—monsters in fact, although of a particular kind. The reason for this state of affairs stems—at least partially—from the fact that the libretto is a trimmed-down version of a preexisting play by Hugo von Hofmannsthal. It was a first collaboration between the composer and librettist, and afterward Hofmannsthal would create his texts for Strauss to order. In their later works on Greek subjects, as you will see, Strauss and Hofmannsthal sought to humanize these mythical beings and treat them more or less as normal people with (relatively) normal problems.

Ariadne auf Naxos (1912–16)

Major Characters: *Ariadne/the Prima Donna (in the Prologue) (soprano); Bacchus/the Tenor (in the Prologue) (tenor);* Commedia dell'arte players: *Zerbinetta (coloratura soprano); Harlequin (baritone); Scaramuccio (tenor); Truffaldino (bass); Brighella (tenor);* In the Prologue: *the Composer (soprano or mezzo-soprano); the Music Master (baritone); the Dancing Master (tenor); the Majordomo (speaking role)*

Scoring: 2 piccolos, 2 flutes, 2 oboes, 2 clarinets, bass clarinet, 2 bassoons, 2 horns, trumpet, trombone, piano, harmonium, celesta, 2 harps, glockenspiel, tambourine, triangle, cymbals, snare drum, bass drum, timpani, 6 violins, 4 violas, 4 cellos, 2 basses

This process begins in their very next collaboration on a Greek subject, *Ariadne auf Naxos*, one of the richest and most complex works that Strauss ever created. There is so much going on in this piece that it's difficult to know where to begin. *Ariadne* is not just a "Greek" opera. It partakes equally of another of Strauss' favorite topics: Old Vienna in the classical period, for this is an opera about an opera. Indeed, it is a comic opera about *two* operas presented simultaneously, one serious, the other comic. Operas about operas are nothing new. Both Mozart (*Der Schauspieldirektor*, or *The Impresario*) and Gluck (*Le Cinesi*, or *The Chinese Women*) wrote them.

In Strauss' opera, the richest man in Vienna holds a soirée for his friends during which the tragedy of Ariadne and a commedia dell'arte farce will be performed. This looks to make for a very long evening, and since the much-anticipated fireworks show must conclude the evening's festivities promptly at 9:00 p.m., the master of the house demands that the two operas be combined so as to save time. The idealistic young composer, the snooty prima donna, and all of the "serious" artists are horrified at having to share the stage with low-class vaudeville performers. This introductory business takes place in the prologue, while the second part consists of the actual opera performance, with its mixture of serious and comic elements.

Ariadne has become famous in music for her celebrated lament. If you know your mythology, you will recall that she was the daughter of King Minos of Crete (of the Minotaur fame). She fell in love with Theseus and assisted him in defeating the Minotaur, departing with him only to be abandoned on the island of Naxos. This is where the lament comes in, as she disconsolately yearns for death, and this is where Strauss' true opera begins in the second part, with Ariadne's "Es gibt ein Reich" ("There is a kingdom"). Ariadne's plight featured previously in numerous musical settings, including an opera by Monteverdi, of which only the lament survives, and a cantata by Haydn, *Arianna a Naxos*.

Because of the necessity of cramming two separate entertainments into a single space, Strauss has a dramatic justification for cutting the Ariadne story down to its most basic elements. All that happens in the opera is that Ariadne sits in her cave praying for death to take her, the picture of noble suffering, until the god Bacchus arrives. He has just escaped from a miserable affair with the witch Circe, who seduces men and then turns them into animals. With Circe unable to work her dark magic on a god, the two had a spat and Bacchus fled, miserable. Ariadne at first mistakes him for Death come to claim her, but the two awaken to a new love that rekindles Ariadne's will to live and leads Bacchus to realize, paraphrasing Mel Brooks, that "It's good to be a god." With its abbreviated plot and absolute minimum of characters (two plus a trio of nymphs as a chorus), Strauss' conception of the Ariadne story is pure Gluck of the "reform" operas, *Orfeo* especially.

Into this slender but relentlessly serious episode the commedia dell'arte characters—the sexy, sassy Zerbinetta and her cohorts—unsuccessfully attempt to harass Ariadne out of her depression. The term *commedia dell'arte* is actually shorthand for "the comedy of artistic improvisation." Arising in Italy sometime during the sixteenth century, it consists of a group of stock characters improvising humorous sketches based on standard situations. The English "Punch and Judy" puppet show grew out of this tradition, and in *Ariadne auf Naxos* the comic characters eventually enact a farce about Zerbinetta being wooed by various suitors. She represents the antithesis of Ariadne: a fun-loving girl who flits from lover to lover, avoiding commitment of any kind. In the prologue, the young composer—a male role designed to be sung by a mezzo-soprano—falls in love with her, with predictably (for him) disappointing results. This mixture of comic and serious glances back to Mozart's *The Magic Flute*, and not for the last time in Strauss' operatic output.

Refusing to take Ariadne's situation seriously, after her lament Zerbinetta tells her to lighten up in possibly the longest and most thrilling coloratura aria in the entire operatic repertoire, "Großmächtige Prinzessin" ("Mighty Princess"). It's a real showstopper, an attempt on Strauss' part to outdo the celebrated arias in Mozart's *Flute* for the Queen of the Night. Zerbinetta herself belongs to a long line of earthy, lower-class female servant characters found in classical-period comic operas, and although *The Magic Flute* may have inspired her music, her personality most closely fits that of the cynical, worldly maid Despina from Mozart's *Così fan tutte*. Unable to appreciate the value of true love and the commitment that it entails, she is ultimately dumbfounded by Ariadne's progress from misery to happiness.

Musically, *Ariadne auf Naxos* is one of Strauss' most sophisticated and, yes, "modern" scores. His use of a chamber orchestra, combined with the neoclassical aesthetic of much of the music, precedes similar works by Stravinsky, Respighi, and the twentieth-century French school by several years. Strauss seldom receives credit for this innovation, because it wasn't followed up systematically in the works that followed and because, as I have already suggested, Strauss' personal brand of neoclassicism was not a self-conscious reversion to an earlier style but rather a natural outgrowth of his own understanding of his place within the German tradition. Also, Strauss just plain loved music that was "referential," whether the reference was Mozart, Wagner, or even his own earlier works. It was a game he played with delight throughout his entire career.

The mixture of styles in *Ariadne*, from the serious to the comic, and taking in the "real life" drama of the Prologue, offered Strauss an unparalleled opportunity to explore the relationship between music and text, varying the dramatic pacing to an unprecedented extent. The style of word setting ranges from the spoken role of the Majordomo in the Prologue to Zerbinetta's coloratura spectacular, where the music completely takes over in the form of insane vocal acrobatics. In between we have the more straightforward lyricism of Ariadne's lament and final duet with Bacchus, as well as the folk-like song-and-dance music of the comic characters. All of this is reflected in the scoring: Ariadne is accompanied mostly by strings and brass, with harp, while Zerbinetta's troupe performs to more prominent woodwinds and percussion.

Of course, these are all tendencies, not strict rules. Strauss' scoring colors his scenes, just as a painter can choose certain tints to highlight a composition without necessarily excluding all of the others. This approach also suits the schizophrenic character of the opera's second part particularly well, the alternation of different kinds of music providing a natural and wholly satisfying formal outline. That said, *Ariadne* is yet another one of those Strauss pieces that lasts about ten minutes longer than it probably needs to. The final duet has no purpose other than to afford the main characters the opportunity to stand and sing.

Dramatically, it has little point; musically, it is one of the highlights of the work. In the contest between text and music at the heart of every operatic setting, you might say that the text wins in the prologue, and the music wins in the opera, but in this case, at least, the whole work wins in the end.

Now for a bit of housekeeping: there are two versions of this opera. The original, composed in 1912, was intended as a short divertissement following Hofmannsthal's recasting of French playwright Molière's play *Le bourgeois gentilhomme* (in German, *Der Bürger als Edelmann*). Intended to last only thirty minutes or so, it wound up typically playing for an hour and a half and, attached to the play, made for an extremely long evening satisfying to neither theater fans nor opera lovers. Strauss composed the incidental music for the play, and that will be discussed in the next chapter. In order to salvage the opera, Hofmannsthal wrote a new prologue, and this is the standard version performed today (and just described). However, the original conception has been making a comeback lately. In the opera proper, the differences between the two are not huge, but the earlier work contains an even longer and more intricate version of Zerbinetta's "coloratura aria from hell."

Die Ägyptische Helena (The Egyptian Helen) (1928)

Major Characters: Helena (Helen of Troy) (soprano); Menelaus, her husband (tenor); Aithra, an Egyptian sorceress (soprano); Altair (baritone); Da-Ud, his son (tenor); the Omniscient Seashell (alto)

Scoring: 2 piccolos, 4 flutes, 2 oboes, English horn, 3 clarinets, bass clarinet, 3 bassoons, contrabassoon, 6 horns, 6 trumpets, 3 trombones, tuba, celesta, organ, 2 harps, glockenspiel, cymbals, bass drum, tam-tam, snare drum, timpani, 16 first violins, 14 second violins, 10 violas, 10 cellos, 8 basses

Onstage: 6 oboes, 6 clarinets, 4 horns, 2 trumpets, 4 trombones, 4 triangles, 2 tambourines, wind machine, timpani

Strauss' next Greek opera, *Die Ägyptische Helena*, is one of his strangest yet most beautiful works. Even in an output rich in glorious writing for his female leads, Helen's act 2 solo, "Zweite Brautnacht" ("Second Wedding Night"), stands out as something special. It is certainly one of the most exquisite pieces ever written for the soprano voice. With an arching vocal line that rides over the orchestra in glorious waves of tone, the music captures perfectly Helen's ecstatic happiness at being reunited with her husband. Indeed, the vocal writing throughout the opera is particularly lovely, if still extremely difficult for the singers, even by Strauss' exacting standards. The scoring, though for large orchestra, is remarkably discreet, never covering the voices, and the instrumental textures have a simplicity and lucidity quite new in his noncomic stage works.

Between *Ariadne* of 1912–16 and *Die Ägyptische Helena* of 1928, Strauss composed two other operas, also on the subject of the difficulties associated with marriage, *Die Frau ohne Schatten* and *Intermezzo*, with *Helena* coming last. *Intermezzo*, in particular, marked a new phase in Strauss' treatment of words and music, the text being handled with greater naturalness of pacing than ever before. That opera is a comedy, while *Helena*, despite a comic initial concept, is not, although it's not a tragedy either. It is rather what you might call a "lyric drama," or something of that sort, but the point is that Strauss never forgot the lessons learned in creating *Intermezzo*, and something of its easy and fluent momentum remains audible here. The difference is that much of the musical invention in the earlier work went into the symphonic interludes between scenes; here it all goes into the vocal line. This makes the opera a voice lover's delight.

What those voices sing about, however, remains a bit of a puzzle. Now, please let me state up front: there is no cheaper shot to take at an opera than to call it a failure on account of its libretto. The only way properly to evaluate any example of the genre is to see it well staged and assess how it works as theater. There is absolutely nothing wrong with *Helena* as music, and as theater the piece offers numerous opportunities for vivid staging, from the opening shipwreck onward. However, the work has been so infrequently performed that taking it in whole is almost impossible, nor has it been recorded with unqualified success. More significantly, it is almost never correctly described, even in some of the scholarly literature.

It is true that Hugo von Hofmannsthal, the librettist, had a certain love of complex language (whether in German or in translation) and a fascination not only with questions of love and fidelity, but also memory, and this last issue especially takes what is basically a simple story and makes it far more complicated than it needs to be. But once we understand how *Helena* differs from the original myth on which it is based, much that would otherwise seem obscure becomes a lot clearer. So let's take a look at the story in more detail, because Strauss' music, two acts of it lasting only a bit more than two hours, really does speak for itself.

The mythical Helen of Troy was allegedly the daughter of Zeus and Leda—as in the legend Leda and the Swan, the form in which Zeus appeared to her. She was married to Menelaus, king of Sparta and brother to Agamemnon, of *Elektra* fame. Helen fell in love and ran away with Paris (*Paris and Helen* being a "reform" opera of Gluck, by the way), leaving her husband and daughter Hermione behind, thus starting the Trojan War. *Helena* is accordingly a family drama related, however distantly, to *Elektra*, and this no doubt accounts in some degree for Strauss' initial interest in it as an operatic subject.

However, one version of the myth states that the gods took pity on Menelaus and replaced the real Helen with a sort of Stepford wife–style android or clone, whisking the real one off to Egypt for safekeeping. This version of the legend is the source of Hofmannsthal's story, but his take on the myth is actually quite different. Specifically, there is only one Helen; but Menelaus, who when the opera begins is returning home from the war with his wife and is ready to kill her for her infidelity, is led to think that there are two. This is the source of much of the confusion that surrounds the plot. Let us ignore the notion that the entire Trojan War was a big waste of time if Menelaus fought it merely to capture Helen so that he could kill her on the way home.

Hofmannsthal's scenario actually owes a lot to Shakespeare's *The Tempest*. In the play, there is an island inhabited by a sorcerer and his minions, but given Strauss' love of the female voice in this case it's a sorceress, a worshiper of Poseidon, named Aithra. She is also an Egyptian princess, not that this matters. Poseidon has given her an all-knowing prophecy-speaking clam (I wish I were kidding) that tells her of the imminent murder of Helen. Aithra summons up a storm, which wrecks the ship. Menelaus, who is very conflicted about killing Helen to begin with, saves her from drowning so that he can think about stabbing her later. Aithra decides that she has to find a way to save Helen as well as her marriage.

So just as Prospero, the sorcerer in *The Tempest*, contrives the wedding between Ferdinand and Miranda, Aithra manipulates the situation so as to effect a reconciliation between the already married Helen and Menelaus. In order to do this, she tells Menelaus that the Helen he has been transporting is not the real one, but the android or whatever. She then drugs him with lotus juice, both to keep him calm and block his memories. So he spends much of the rest of the opera both deluded and hallucinating, and generally making very little sense. Aithra also gives Helen a makeover, restoring her original beauty and letting her in on the plan so that the story of there being two of her makes more sense. This, aside from a diversion involving a few elves making Menelaus believe he has killed Helen and Paris all over again, is basically act 1.

Act 2 takes place on an oasis in the Atlas Mountains. Aithra originally offered to send Helen and Menelaus back to Sparta, presumably with a lifetime supply of lotus juice, but Helen asks her to give them some private time to mend their relationship before returning home. However, things aren't going too well on that front. Thanks to those dratted elves, Menelaus believes that he has killed the real Helen and that the made-over one at the oasis is the fake. He also won't drink his lotus juice. At that moment, they are disturbed by the arrival of Altair and his son Da-Ud, sent by Aithra to greet the guests. Both take one look at Helen and immediately determine to claim her. Menelaus, who has been through all of this before, sees Da-Ud as another Paris and, while they are all out hunting together, kills him. Altair doesn't especially care; it just means one less competitor for Helen.

While the hunt is going on (offstage), Aithra shows up to express relief that Helen hasn't yet broken into her store of lotus juice, since Aithra's servant accidentally included a flask of remembrance tonic as well. However, to her surprise, Helen says that she's had it with Aithra's well-meaning intervention and needs Menelaus to accept her as she is, with all of her faults and limitations. She's done with dissembling (but she'll keep the makeover). Menelaus, for his part, still believes that he has killed the real Helen and, full of remorse, resolves to take the remembrance potion, believing that it is poison. Both of them drink together. Menelaus comes to his senses, sees Helen for herself, and understands that he must accept her accordingly. At Aithra's command, Altair withdraws, and their daughter Hermione joins them, a family reunited.

You would be perfectly justified in finding this whole thing a hopelessly contrived and ridiculous way of making the obvious point that a successful marriage must be based on the realistic acceptance of each partner's good and bad qualities, but the topic meant a lot to Strauss and Hofmannsthal—so much so that they both lavished a tremendous amount of care and craft illustrating the point. Strauss adored this story, and this opera. Nor is *Helena* unusual in spending a great deal of time on something that could have been resolved in maybe five minutes of normal conversation. Opera, obviously, is not normal conversation, and *Helena* offers an object lesson in how a wholly stylized and artificial medium can be used to tell a story about the exact opposite: the need for realism, understanding, and acceptance—or failing that, buckets of lotus juice.

Daphne (1938)

Major Characters: Daphne (soprano); Peneios, her father (bass); Gaea, Daphne's mother (alto); Leukippos, a shepherd (tenor); Apollo (tenor)

Scoring: piccolo, 3 flutes, 2 oboes, English horn, 3 clarinets, basset horn, bass clarinet, 3 bassoons, contrabassoon, 4 horns, 3 trumpets, 3 trombones, tuba, 2 harps, bass drum, cymbals, triangle, tambourine, tam-tam, timpani, 16 first violins, 16 second violins, 12 violas, 10 cellos, 8 basses

Onstage: organ, alphorn

After the complexities of *Helena*, Strauss' next mythological opera, *Daphne*, may come as something of a relief. The plot is simplicity itself: Daphne, who loves nature above all, rejects any possible romantic relationships, even one with the god Apollo, who rashly kills her mortal suitor and childhood friend Leukippos and then, out of guilt, has Zeus turn her into a laurel tree so that she will never be parted from the natural world that she so adores. That's it. The whole work consists of a single act lasting a bit more than ninety minutes. Strauss called the opera "A Bucolic Tragedy," with the tragedy residing in the fact that because Daphne cannot form any lasting personal attachments, she loses her humanity entirely.

As for the "bucolic" moniker, that refers both to the pastoral setting and to the sound of the score. The work opens with a gently lyrical passage for woodwind ensemble: oboe, English horn, clarinet, basset horn, and bassoons. This is exactly the kind of music that, since time immemorial, has been used to evoke rural scenes. So iconic are these sonorities that, as I mentioned in discussing the tone poems, some of the instruments that produce them were banned from nineteenth-century symphonic music—notably the English horn—because of their pictorial associations. Here, they often lead the ensemble.

Strauss treats this simple tale with the formal clarity that it deserves. The entire work resembles a large movement in sonata form. Its exposition has two subjects (or scenes): an introduction (chorus of shepherds) followed by the scene between Daphne and Leukippos. The second subject consists of Daphne's meeting with Apollo and her rejection of him. For the development section, we have the festival in which Leukippos appears disguised as a woman in order to dance with Daphne, his unmasking by Apollo, Daphne's final rejection of them both, and Apollo's jealous murder of Leukippos. It is a true "development," the dramatic heart of the opera where all of the characters (and their music) interact dynamically. Daphne's lament, Apollo's sorrow, and her transformation scene serve as the recapitulation and coda.

This scenario really does show how classical sonata form makes purely orchestral music dramatic. *Daphne* requires ninety minutes because it has a story to tell in words, and, if it is to make any kind of sense, this requires time. If you were to take the words out, then what you would have left would be two subjects in contrasted keys, their development, and a restatement in the home key to provide a satisfying resolution—in other words, a symphonic first movement. The purely instrumental drama takes much less time because untexted music can move far more quickly than music with words, without losing coherence. It needs no intervening verbal explanation to make logical sense, but the formal principles are identical.

Daphne's concluding "transformation scene" (CD Track 2) has become one of Strauss' most highly regarded operatic moments, often performed separately in concert. Strauss jokingly claimed that he cribbed the diaphanous string textures at 9:36 from Wagner's "Magic Fire Music" in *Die Walküre*, but the sound is actually quite different. Initially, Daphne sings of her joy at becoming one with the woodland creatures that she loves above all else, but as her metamorphosis continues, she gradually loses her ability to speak and, after a gently lyrical and rhapsodic orchestral interlude, she becomes at last the wordless voice of nature herself. It's gorgeous, it's hypnotic, and it almost didn't happen at all.

Daphne was originally intended as part of a double bill, the antithesis of the antiwar opera *Friedenstag*. That piece ends with a grand choral apotheosis, and the librettist, Joseph Gregor, projected the same for *Daphne* in order to unify the two. Strauss didn't like the idea but couldn't quite put his finger on the problem until conductor Clemens Krauss pointed out that having a bunch of people standing around singing at a tree was absurd. Strauss agreed and came up with the idea for the current final scene, once again showing a concern for "realism" quite different from what we usually imagine that term to mean, but equally logical in its own way.

Of all of Strauss' late operas, many critics agree that *Daphne* deserves to be the one most frequently revived. Standing in the way is the fact that it contains not one but two lead tenor roles, Leukippos and Apollo, something unheard-of in Strauss but a fact that may make the piece more pleasing to audiences accustomed to heroic tenor leads. Of course, this being Strauss, the two parts are both extremely strenuous, especially since much of the music is not declamatory but requires sustained, lyrical, dynamically nuanced singing. Strauss' twist on the traditional pairing of soprano and tenor voices, one that helps makes the work so interesting, is that this particular soprano isn't terribly interested in either of them. So there is no conventional love duet, but the contest for Daphne between the two of them is vocally thrilling.

Daphne's directness and uncomplicated expressiveness make it easy to stage, while the concluding transformation scene shows that Strauss really did save the best for last. This coda, though soft and serene, is not one of those lyrical appendices that starts after the story stops. On the contrary, it reveals an unassailable musical and dramatic logic, and this, combined with the opera's relative brevity and lack of pretention, shows that Strauss was not running out of steam as he aged. Indeed, his next (and last) Greek opera, *Die Liebe der Danae*, starts from strength and never lets up.

Die Liebe der Danae (Danae's Love) (1940)

Major Characters: Pollux, King of Eos (tenor); Danae, his daughter (soprano); Jupiter (baritone); Merkur (Mercury) (tenor); Midas, King of Lydia (tenor)

Scoring: 3 piccolos, 3 flutes, 2 oboes, English horn, 3 clarinets, basset horn, bass clarinet, 3 bassoons, contrabassoon, 6 horns, 4 trumpets, 4 trombones, tuba, 2 harps, celesta, piano, glockenspiel, tambourine, triangle, cymbals, bass drum, snare drum, tam-tam, timpani, 16 first violins, 16 second violins, 12 violas, 10 cellos, 8 basses

In Greek mythology, Princess Danae was the mother of Perseus, after being impregnated by Zeus (Jupiter). He appeared to her as a shower of gold—I know, and we're not going there—and there really isn't much more to the old legend than that. She is merely another one of Jupiter's many conquests. Strauss' take on this story is delightfully funny and touching, and illustrates more clearly than any of his other Greek operas just how tellingly he was able to humanize these old tales and populate them with emotionally true, sympathetic characters.

As Strauss and his librettist Joseph Gregor tell it, Danae's dad, King Pollux, is in big trouble with his creditors. To solve his money problems, he agrees to marry off his daughter to King Midas—he of the "golden touch." However, Jupiter, who has been sending Danae dreams of gold, has arranged to appear disguised as Midas so that his jealous wife, Juno, doesn't get wind of his latest amorous exploits. The real Midas pretends to be his own humble messenger and gift bearer, so that Jupiter can make a quick switch if Juno finds out that he's up to something naughty. The comic element consists primarily of Pollux being chased around by his creditors, and in Jupiter being hounded by the four queens with whom he previously had affairs and who are now Danae's jealous maidens-in-waiting.

Jupiter has threatened Midas by telling him that unless he cooperates, he will lose his golden touch and spend the rest of his life as he started it: as a poor Syrian donkey driver. Danae, however, falls in love with the real Midas. During their love scene in act 2, he accidentally embraces her in an excess of enthusiasm and turns her into a golden statue. Jupiter shows up and demands her love, but when she and Midas oppose him (naturally the statue speaks), Midas loses his magic touch; Danae returns to life, and both of them wind up poor but happy in a low-rent hut in Syria. Jupiter makes one last attempt to win Danae over, but she refuses with great dignity and charm, persuading him that Midas' love is worth more to her than riches, and Jupiter leaves sadly with the realization that he will never experience the human affection he craves.

The music that Strauss created for this story is remarkable. For Pollux and his creditors, he has adopted a style very close to that of Kurt Weill and the Berlin cabaret of the 1920s: a dry, witty, conversationally paced music that would not sound out of place in Weill and Brecht's *The Rise and Fall of the City of Mahagonny*. Strauss actually found this idiom much earlier, in *Intermezzo*, and he developed it further in *Die schweigsame Frau*, but since those operas are as little known as this one, he seldom gets the credit he deserves for this thoroughly modern and very deft sort of comic "business."

The more lyrical writing for the three participants in the Jupiter–Midas–Danae love triangle is of course vintage Strauss, but the final duet between Jupiter and Danae is something new. Jupiter is arguably Strauss' finest—and most exhausting—baritone role. The god is a complete character: arrogant, bullying, harassed, lonely, wistful, and ultimately cowed by Danae's love for Midas. The closing scene consists neither of languishing love music (as in *Ariadne*) nor a triumphant apotheosis (as in *Helena*), but is rather a vigorous dialogue between two strong, well-matched personalities. It moves with an almost muscular strength and purpose, and one immediately senses the conviction, the sincerity that Strauss put into composing it.

Indeed, Strauss was very much in a "summing up" frame of mind when working on *Danae*. He thought it would be his last opera, not just because of his age, but also because of the era's dismal wartime situation. Initially, he insisted that the opera be performed only two years after the cessation of hostilities, but in the event he had an opportunity to hear the work at a dress rehearsal in Salzburg in 1944. The actual premiere took place three years after his death, in 1952. It may be for that reason that the work never really stood a chance to enter the repertoire, but there were others worth mentioning as well.

By the late 1940s, Strauss' reputation both as a composer and as a person had hit an all-time low. Musically, he had long been regarded as a bygone representative of an outdated, romantic aesthetic. His late works were considered to be hopelessly passé, and his public persona had been irreparably damaged by his relationship with the Nazi regime. Driven in part by bad judgment, in part by opportunism, and in part by the need to protect his Jewish daughter-in-law and grandchildren, he had done some very foolish things and had made a lot of enemies in the 1930s and 1940s, and consequently attracted a great deal of bad press and ill will from people who, rightly or wrongly, found plenty of ammunition to feed their hostility.

In the midst of all this private and public commotion—including the rise of the postwar musical avant-garde and the Nazi destruction of German civilization—Strauss had the nerve to write a comedy about the value of love over money. And this coming from a composer regularly lambasted for his reputation as a greedy materialist. It was too much. The quality of the music and effectiveness of the treatment were completely irrelevant. *Die Liebe der Danae* was doomed from the outset, despite which it turned out not be his last opera. That was *Capriccio*, widely acknowledged by Strauss connoisseurs to be a masterpiece, thus further precluding *Danae* from being rehabilitated even as a glorious "last gasp." It is an irony that needs to be redressed.

Finally, conductor Clemens Krauss assembled a brief suite from music in the opera's second and third acts, calling it "Symphonic Fragment from *Die Liebe der Danae*." It is very pretty, even if like many other Strauss opera excerpts it begins with a bang only to peter out toward the end. It's only about twelve minutes long. Another of the reasons these late Greek operas may have suffered in popularity has been the lack of concert extracts that sell them effectively to the listening public. I have already noted how *Daphne* got a boost from separate performances and recordings of its concluding transformation scene, and it's a pity that neither *Helena* nor *Danae* have benefitted from similar treatment.

The 1944 general rehearsal in Salzburg, the only time that Strauss was able to hear the opera during his lifetime, was a very sad occasion for him. It was played as part of the festivities celebrating his eightieth birthday, with World War II at its height. Toward the end of the performance, he stood up until the music stopped and then thanked the artists, saying, "Perhaps we shall all meet again in a better place." Then he left the hall.

Old Vienna (and Paris)
Der Rosenkavalier, Le bourgeois gentilhomme, Schlagobers, Couperin Suites, Arabella, and Capriccio

Der Rosenkavalier (The Knight of the Rose) (1911)

Major Characters: The Marschallin, Princess Marie Thérèse von Werdenberg (soprano); Octavian, Count Rofrano, her lover (mezzo-soprano); Baron Ochs auf Lerchenau (bass); Sophie von Faninal (soprano); Herr von Faninal, Sophie's father (baritone); an Italian tenor

Scoring: piccolo, 3 flutes, 3 oboes, English horn, 3 clarinets, basset horn, bass clarinet, 3 bassoons, contrabassoon, 4 horns, 3 trumpets, 3 trombones, tuba, bass drum, cymbals, triangle, tambourine, glockenspiel, large cog rattle, large tenor drum, snare drum, sleigh bells, castanets, celesta, 2 harps, timpani, 16 first violins, 16 second violins, 12 violas, 10 cellos, 8 basses

Stage band: 2 flutes, oboe, 3 clarinets, 2 bassoons, 2 horns, trumpet, snare drum, harmonium, piano, strings (either solo or in multiples greater than 2)

Strauss was no more capable of repeating the hard-hitting, revolutionary achievement of *Elektra* than Stravinsky was able to write a second *Rite of Spring*. Both works represent singular moments in their respective composers' lives. However, Stravinsky's refusal to remain stuck in a stylistic rut receives praise as an example of his capacity for aesthetic renewal, whereas Strauss is often castigated for living up to his name (*Strauss* means "ostrich" in German) and sticking his head in the musical sand with the composition of his next opera, *Der Rosenkavalier*. What accounts for this double standard? Is it fair?

The short answer is "No," it is not fair, nor is it correct. In the first place, as an operatic composer Strauss adapted his style to the subject. In order to continue writing along the lines he established in *Elektra*, he would have needed a story that required similar musical treatment. He might well have found one. There was no shortage of decadent psychodramas in turn-of-the-century Europe, and his colleagues, such as Schreker, Korngold, Zemlinsky, and later Berg, turned them into often gut-wrenching operas with great relish and remarkable success. But this was not the direction in which Strauss wanted to go, nor did he view it as his principal strength as a composer.

Just as significantly, however—and this goes directly to Strauss' challenge in creating a "school" of German opera—German musical culture was not inherently theatrical. Those aspects of it that did embrace opera and ballet were largely Italian or French. Stravinsky's musical revolutions took place in the field of ballet. He was not subject to German notions of symphonic process or aesthetic purity. Wagner spent a good bit of his career justifying himself on the basis that the symphony was "dead," and that he was therefore the logical successor to Beethoven. Strauss operated under no such illusions. Far more even than Wagner, his allegiance lay with theatrical music as a valid pursuit all its own, and he gave his loyalty fully to the work at hand, adapting to the needs of the moment while adhering broadly to his personal view of the German symphonic tradition. He was not out to change it, merely to redefine it effectively as a theatrical medium.

So when the opportunity came to create an original comedy, set in the Vienna of Mozart's and Gluck's time, Strauss jumped at the chance. After all, his favorite composer was Mozart, and he believed his own strongest gifts lay in the sort of sensual comedy of manners best illustrated by Mozart's three great Italian operas to librettos by Lorenzo Da Ponte: *The Marriage of Figaro, Don Giovanni*, and *Così fan tutte*. Mozart's operas are not "reform" works in the manner of Gluck's, although they were strongly influenced by them and had much the same effect. They are simply Mozart's operas, unique in their musical richness, elegance, wit, expressive range, emotional truth, coherence, melodic abundance, and perfection of dramatic pacing.

All of Strauss' operas set in Enlightenment Vienna or France thus owe something to Mozart, just as the Greek works often harken back to Gluck. They are very much "mythological" operas too, in the sense that they recall a time composed of as much fantasy as fact. The presentation of the silver rose in the betrothal ceremony in *Der Rosenkavalier* was purely Strauss and Hofmannsthal's invention. Strauss' use of the waltzes that have made the opera famous, and forever after confused his name with that of the Viennese "Waltz King" Johann Strauss Jr. (they were not related), is wholly anachronistic. The waltz did not become a popular dance craze until at least half a century after Mozart's death.

In other words, Strauss and Hofmannsthal manufactured a new mythological realm for this specific series of works. Let's call it "Enlightenment Europe." Strauss then brought this half-real, half-fantastic period to life with its own original musical idiom, a complex amalgam of eighteenth-century elegance and polish, nineteenth-century dance rhythm and symphonic construction, and a deftly modern approach to harmony and orchestral technique. *Der Rosenkavalier* is thus not less "advanced" than *Elektra*. It is merely less dissonant, and to define musical progress primarily as a function of harmonic procedure, as so many commentators do, strikes me as unacceptably facile, especially in the inherently heterogeneous world of opera.

Knowing Mozart's *The Marriage of Figaro* definitely adds an extra dimension to your enjoyment of *Der Rosenkavalier*. The character of the Marschallin, for example, is obviously modeled on the Countess in Mozart's opera. *Marschallin*, incidentally, is German for the "wife of the Field Marshal," her real name being Princess Marie Thérèse von Werdenberg. Both women share a poignant awareness of time passing and of the loss of their youth. However, there is a crucial difference, in that Mozart's Countess laments the loss of her husband's love, while the Marschallin, who is no less gracious and intelligent, knows that she soon will have to forfeit the attentions of her much younger lover. She suffers from no moral qualms on account of her affair—only the usual concern for discretion. Her husband never appears in the opera at all.

The Marschallin's lover, Octavian, is what's called in the opera business a "trouser" role, or a male character sung by a woman. The most famous of these is Mozart's Cherubino in *Figaro*, but we must also keep in mind the musically even more relevant Prince Orlovsky in Johann Strauss Jr.'s very Viennese operetta *Die Fledermaus*. This convention permits composers to differentiate vocally very young men from the other male characters, and it adds a sexually titillating androgynous element to emotionally charged situations. Strauss loved it; Hofmannsthal loathed it, but later, as part of the deal between the two in setting to music the *Prologue* to the revised *Ariadne*, Strauss allocated the male character of the composer to the female voice as well. In *Der Rosenkavalier*, this means that three out of the four leads are sopranos, Strauss' favorite voice type, and he takes full advantage of this in the closing trio and duet.

The exception, Baron Ochs, is a baritone, but Strauss pays sly homage to the traditional Italian tenor lead by introducing an actual Italian tenor into the Marschallin's boudoir to sing a wonderfully exaggerated fake bel canto aria, "Di rigori armato," in act 1. As with the later waltzes, the style of the music, which is intensely romantic and deadly serious, has absolutely nothing to do with the ostensible period in which the action of the opera takes place—a very "in" bit of musical humor, this—but it never sounds incongruous in its context. It is just part of the larger sound world that is *Der Rosenkavalier*.

Most comic operas have the same plot: overcoming the barriers to an eventual marriage. Even where this isn't the main plot, as in Verdi's *Falstaff*, it's the subplot. *Der Rosenkavalier* is no exception. The loutish Baron Ochs plans to marry Sophie von Faninal. His cousin, the Marschallin, suggests that her lover Octavian be hired to present the traditional silver rose of betrothal to Sophie. Ochs agrees. When Octavian meets Sophie, they fall madly in love and, with the aid of the Marschallin (and just about everyone else), devise a scheme to humiliate Ochs so that the two of them can marry. Both the Marschallin and Faninal accept the inevitable.

The plot may be straightforward, but *Der Rosenkavalier* is a very long opera, usually lasting between three and a quarter and three and a half hours, uncut. It is full of highlights, including the following:

- The Marschallin's act 1 monologue, in which she sings about how she sometimes stops the clocks in the house so as not to be reminded of time passing and age advancing.
- The tenor aria, a pastiche in the Italian style that parodies but at the same time pays affectionate tribute to early nineteenth-century composers Bellini and Donizetti.

- The first act's conclusion. As the Marschallin prepares to leave for church, she realizes that one day she will lose Octavian despite his protestations of undying love for her. The music is saturated with nostalgia, Strauss repeatedly asking the strings for a rich, vibrato sonority.

- The Presentation of the Rose scene in act 2, with its crystalline orchestration for flutes, harps, celesta, and solo violins—the disorienting harmonies a perfect evocation of awaking love between Sophie and Octavian.

- The waltz episodes in the same act.

- Finally, in act 3, the concluding trio for the Marschallin, Sophie, and Octavian, in which the three soprano voices create an unforgettable tapestry of interweaving melodic lines. The trio evolves into the duet "Ist ein Traum" ("It's a Dream") (CD Track 3), as Sophie and Octavian, lost to the world, acknowledge their love for each other while the Marschallin looks on with a bittersweet mixture of sadness and understanding. "It is always this way with the youngsters," Faninal tells her, to which the Marschallin graciously signals her acceptance and bids farewell to Octavian with a short, simple, but somehow emotionally devastating, "Yes, yes" ("Ja, ja"). The tipsy "young love" theme from the Presentation of the Rose scene then returns to usher in the opera's closing pages.

The opera's length is necessary to get through Hofmannsthal's literarily exquisite libretto, thereby illustrating the fact that superb literature is not necessarily compatible with superb opera. Wagner's operas, for instance, are so long because he was a much less able writer than he was a composer and the composer couldn't edit the writer. Strauss was not so handicapped; he confessed that the work had its less effective moments but admitted that he was so in love with the libretto that he just couldn't stop. *Der Rosenkavalier* is the operatic *locus classicus* for a Strauss piece where the plot ends, and then everyone stands still and sings some of the best music in the entire work for fifteen or twenty minutes longer than necessary. It has also been pointed out that the third-act humiliation of Ochs is rather cruel and somewhat crude slapstick, but that seems to be a function of German humor, similar to the sort of thing we find in Till Eulenspiegel's merry trial and hanging. Given Hofmannsthal's sharp and witty libretto, the elements of physical humor inevitably come down to questions of personal taste.

The music too tends to divide opinion. Some listeners find the work sickeningly sweet, while others love its overt sentimentality and delight in sensuous sounds. The opening is pure sex music of the kind that Strauss excelled in, and which really never has been equaled in its graphic depiction of the act itself. There is a difference between "love music" and "sex music." Wagner drew the line in *Tristan und Isolde*: the hypnotic second-act "Liebesnacht" ("Love Night") is love music, while Isolde's orgasmic concluding "Liebestod" ("Love Death") is sex music, even though it's all in her head because Tristan has just died. *Der Rosenkavalier* opens with sex music and ends with love music, just the opposite of Wagner's process, and a telling point of contrast between the two composers' philosophies. Wagner's sex is tragic and transcendental; Strauss' is fun and physical, with gleefully whooping horns celebrating at the climax.

Nevertheless, whatever one's view of the work as a whole, most critics and listeners agree that in the Marschallin, Strauss has created one of the greatest female character portraits in all of opera, and that is saying a lot. A great singing actress can steal the show with a less-than-stellar voice on the basic of intelligence and nuance alone. It's that kind of a role, and for this reason the opera has been a favorite of sopranos since the time of its premiere, especially those nearing retirement who have neither the vocal nor physical qualifications to spend their remaining time, as Anna Russell memorably said, "dying at the top of their lungs of TB." The character's glamour, wistfulness, grace, dignity, and rueful bittersweetness is composed right into the music and remains an astonishing achievement.

Another testament to *Der Rosenkavalier*'s enduring viability is the popularity of the concert suites that Strauss arranged from the music. There are no less than three of them, two sets of waltzes and a longer work of about twenty minutes assembled from various highlights throughout the three acts. The opera was even turned into a silent film, for which Strauss arranged the entire score to be played by a cinema pit orchestra. *Der Rosenkavalier* may not be Strauss' most "perfect" score, whatever that means, but there is little question that it is musically his most gushingly abundant.

Le bourgeois gentilhomme (1912; Suite: 1920)

Scoring: 2 piccolos, 2 flutes, 2 oboes, 2 clarinets, 2 bassoons, 2 horns, trumpet, trombone, glockenspiel, snare drum, tambourine, triangle, bass drum, cymbals, harp, piano, timpani, 6 violins, 4 violas, 4 cellos, 2 basses

The stupendous success of *Der Rosenkavalier* must have convinced Strauss that he was on the right track, even as it annoyed his fellow composers and conductors partial to the German avant-garde. His next project, the *Bourgeois gentilhomme / Ariadne auf Naxos* double bill of 1912, seemed guaranteed to annoy them even more. *Ariadne* has already been discussed in the previous chapter, but the orchestral suite that Strauss fashioned in 1920 from his incidental music to Molière / Hofmannsthal's *Le bourgeois gentilhomme* even more tellingly asks the musical question, "When is one actually looking forward by looking back?"

Molière's comedy-ballet of 1670 was originally accompanied by the music of Jean-Baptiste Lully, the composer whose music defined the reign of Louis XIV. Strauss arranged three of Lully's pieces for his own suite, while also quoting Wagner (*Das Rheingold*), Verdi (*Rigoletto*), and even himself (the "sheep" from *Don Quixote*) in the concluding number, "The Dinner," with each quotation standing in for the appropriate course. The play recounts the wealthy M. Jourdain's desperate attempts to join the ranks of the nobility and satirizes both the bourgeoisie and the aristocracy of the day. It's very funny, and even though Hofmannsthal's German retread wasn't very successful, Strauss' contribution has been a favorite repertory item ever since.

The suite is scored basically for the same chamber orchestra forces as *Ariadne*, not surprisingly, although it sounds much closer to the vigorous patter of the Prologue than to the lyrical effulgence of the formal opera. Neoclassical pieces, of which this remains one of the earliest successful examples, pay homage to the baroque and classical periods in music that tends to be busily driven in quick movements, and graciously lyrical or dancelike in slower tempos. Rhythms tend to be clear and straightforward, and formally the music emphasizes simple ABA or rondo (ritornello) structures—ABACA. The aesthetic represents a reaction against the romantic, sentimental style that Strauss had exploited so successfully in *Der Rosenkavalier* as well as the decadent opulence of its predecessors.

The work has nine movements: an overture, a selection of dances and intermezzi, and the final "dinner." Perhaps the most remarkable thing about the music is that three dances borrowed from Lully sound just like the rest and that the entire work sounds like Strauss. One of the hallmarks of great composers is that no matter what idiom they choose, their individual personalities always shine through. Thus, according to this standard, Stravinsky's neoclassical pieces really do still sound like Stravinsky. Prokofiev's *Classical Symphony* sounds unmistakably like Prokofiev. Respighi's neoclassical works, such as *The Birds* or the *Ancient Airs and Dances*, charming and brilliant as they are, do not reveal a similarly strong creative personality.

I have already discussed the fact that Strauss seldom receives the credit that he deserves for the aesthetic advance that this music represents, first because the neoclassical movement originated in France, and second because he did not follow it up consistently or with single-minded persistence. That said, he absorbed the lessons of *Aridane* and *Le bourgeois gentilhomme* thoroughly, and they remain a more important component of Strauss' musical makeup than many commentators willingly admit. In particular, the musical language of the classical period is also the language of opera buffa (comic opera), and the later comedies make full use of the deft scoring, greater simplicity of form and texture, and rapid, almost conversational pacing that typifies the writing in this work.

Le bourgeois gentilhomme remained a great favorite with Strauss. He chose to include it on the program of his eighty-fifth-birthday concert, and it has become a repertory staple of chamber orchestras the world over. He would turn again to vast orchestral forces in the operas to come now and again, but with a newfound lucidity and leanness, and more careful attention to subtleties of balance between voice and orchestra (see the discussion of *Die Ägyptische Helena* in the previous chapter). The domestic comedies *Intermezzo* and *Die schweigsame Frau*, as well as the comic episodes in *Danae*, all breathe a similar air and have their origins in the neoclassical style that Strauss found here for the first time.

Schlagobers (Whipped Cream) (1921–22)

Scoring: piccolo, 4 flutes, 2 oboes, English horn, 4 clarinets, bass clarinet, 4 bassoons, contrabassoon, 4 horns, 3 trumpets (plus 4 onstage), 3 trombones, tuba, glockenspiel, xylophone, cymbals, bass drum, tambourine, snare drum, triangle, castanets, box of sand, 2 harps, celesta, timpani, 12 first and 12 second violins, 8 violas, 8 cellos, 6 basses

Because it contains so much dance music, *Le bourgeois gentilhomme* has also gained fame as a ballet. This is ironic, because Strauss composed two original ballets, both of which stand among his least-known, even most reviled, works. That his relationship to the ballet should have been so conflicted is strange: the operas are full of very effective dance music, starting with Salome's famous "Dance of the Seven Veils," which remains a concert favorite. It is doubly ironic that Strauss' most overt tribute to Vienna, the ballet *Schlagobers* (Whipped Cream), is generally regarded as the absolute nadir of his compositional output. It will be interesting to take a moment to understand why this is so.

There is probably no position in all of music more suicidal than that of music director of the Vienna State Opera. Since Mahler's tenure, which lasted a decade, from 1897 to 1907, no one has managed to hold the post for longer. Compare this to James Levine's career as music director of the Metropolitan Opera in New York, which began formally in 1976 and continues to this day (2014 at time of writing). Since the fall of the Hapsburg monarchy in World War I, Austria as a country has basically consisted of a vast bureaucracy looking for something to run.

The complexity of opera makes its administration inherently bureaucratic. For the Austrians, it is a marriage made in heaven. Meddling in cultural affairs has thus become something of a national pastime, and opera stands at the pinnacle of national culture.

The job of the Vienna State Opera's music director itself offers irresistible temptations: the best soloists accompanied by one of the greatest orchestras in the world, and a historical pedigree second to none. In reality, though, no one has been able to stand it for more than a few years at a time. The constant intrigue, politics, and general aggravation that come with the territory ensure that the position has become one of classical music's great revolving doors. Strauss held it, in a dysfunctional partnership with Franz Schalk (best known as a Bruckner disciple), from 1919 to 1924. It was a difficult time: World War I had left the truncated remains of the empire in economic ruin. Strauss was particularly concerned with preserving the opera's ballet company, arranging and performing works by Schumann, Beethoven, Couperin, and Gluck, among others.

However honorable his intentions, the last thing Vienna wanted was a glitzy, expensive comic ballet extravaganza about kids in a pastry shop where all the goodies come to life and romp around the stage gleefully celebrating all of the treats currently denied the city's starving and miserable residents. Criticism of the mindless scenario, which was Strauss' own, simply won't do. Ballets and operas about toy shops and candy characters come to life were not new, nor would *Schlagobers* be the last of them. One has only to think of Tchaikovsky's *The Nutcracker*, Respighi's *La boutique fantasque*, or Ravel's *L'enfant et les sortilèges*.

The problem with *Schlagobers* was in its timing. Strauss claimed he was just trying to make people happy. Perhaps so, but the people were not in a happy mood. When it came to music Strauss was, in any case, almost completely uninterested in external circumstances, which is remarkable for a composer whose entire mature output took its inspiration from extramusical ideas and imagery. Also, as Germany's leading composer, where Strauss went so, by implication, did German music. The idea that such an unconscionably frivolous piece as *Schlagobers* could be pointing the way forward was simply too horrible to contemplate, and the critics trashed it accordingly. Intended as a crowning achievement to celebrate its composer's sixtieth birthday, *Schlagobers* premiered in 1924, and it is no coincidence that this was also Strauss' last year as music director in Vienna.

Its failure, then, was absolute, and even today the work has a terrible reputation, particularly among those who have never heard it, bolstered by the general contempt in which Strauss' later music has been held historically. It has received very few, rather obscure complete recordings, plus one reasonably current release of the suite that Strauss later extracted from the complete seventy-five-minute work. For this reason, it makes little sense to talk about it more extensively here, but a couple of remarks about the music deserve consideration.

Both the title and the scenario point to the sort of high-calorie musical self-indulgence that makes even some of Strauss' most sympathetic listeners cringe. The temptation, then, is to judge the work on what it seems likely to be, based on past experience, rather than on what it is and how it actually sounds. If you look at the scoring, you will see something very interesting. Specifically, the number of strings, relatively speaking, is small given the abundance of winds, brass, and percussion. This suggests a leaner overall sonority than usual, and so it proves. The music takes full advantage of the simpler textures and sharper profile of Strauss' neoclassical works, even though its general style remains squarely late romantic.

There is a vigorous march featuring the hard-edged xylophone, a number of important woodwind solos to balance out the obligatory solo violin, and a general muscularity and focus on rhythm that tends to counteract one's expectations of decadent fluff. In short, *Schlagobers* is good ballet music, something that cannot be said to the same degree of its predecessor, *Josephs Legende*. There is no need to insist that the work is an undiscovered masterpiece to underscore the notion that Strauss knew what he was doing and grasped that an effective presentation even of this obnoxiously cute scenario required more than kitschy music that risked inducing in its listeners the aural equivalent of a diabetic coma. Perhaps a great new recording will demonstrate the truth of these assertions.

Couperin Suites:
Dance Suite from Keyboard Pieces by François Couperin (1923)
Divertimento, Op. 86 (1940–41)

Scoring: 2 flutes, 2 oboes, English horn, 2 clarinets, 2 bassoons, 2 horns, trumpet, trombone, glockenspiel, tambourine, triangle, bass drum, cymbals, celesta, harp, harpsichord, organ, 4 first violins, 3 second violins, 2 violas, 2 cellos, 1 bass

Far more successful than *Schlagobers* was Strauss' arrangement of harpsichord music by French baroque master François Couperin (1668– 1733). Couperin wrote more than two hundred keyboard pieces that he grouped into suites, or *ordres*, giving many of them fanciful titles (such as "Le Tic-Toc-Choc"). He was unquestionably one of the great- est composers for the keyboard, on a par with Scarlatti and Bach (who admired him). Strauss found his music delightful and arranged selec- tions of keyboard music at two periods, during his tenure in Vienna in the 1920s, and then later in 1940–41 during World War II, at the request of conductor Clemens Krauss.

Krauss in turn put Strauss' two groups of Couperin transcrip- tions together into a longer ballet called *Verklungene Feste* (Bygone Celebrations). Strauss, in turn, took his second set of transcriptions, added a couple more, and published the new work as his *Divertimento: Keyboard Pieces by Couperin for Small Orchestra*, Op. 86. Both pieces rank among Strauss' least-known orchestral/theatrical works, which is simply incomprehensible, as the arrangements are delightful. Again, when Stravinsky did something very similar with music by Pergolesi and other Italian baroque composers and called the result *Pulcinella*, the result was hailed as a masterpiece, but Strauss' work, which is no less accomplished and appealing, simply vanished into musical oblivion.

Part of the explanation is that Stravinsky was based in Paris and had Diaghilev's Ballets Russes to promote his work and thus help him to gain entrée into ballet companies the world over. Strauss had no such advan- tage, nor was he primarily a ballet composer. Nevertheless, in making these arrangements, Strauss anticipated a popular trend in twentieth- century neoclassicism. Conductor Thomas Beecham adapted Handel for his ballet *The Great Elopement*, and the suite *Love in Bath*; William Walton looked to Bach for *The Wise Virgins*; and Alfredo Casella wrote his *Scarlattiana* for piano and chamber orchestra. These are just three examples of many, and there is no reason why Strauss' efforts should be regarded as any less valuable or successful.

The scoring of the two suites is almost identical, with the use of the harpsichord designed to add a period flavor. Curiously, it has just the opposite effect in this context, particularly when it appears in such fantastical combinations as Strauss contrives in the Dance Suite's third-movement "Carillon," which is arranged initially for glockenspiel, harp, celesta, and harpsichord. The sonority is enchanting, but also wholly modern. Happily, these works have been recorded a few times each and shouldn't be too difficult to find, but they are still far less popular than they ought to be.

Arabella (1932)

Major Characters: Arabella (soprano); Zdenka, her sister (soprano); Count Waldner, their father (bass); Adelaide, their mother (mezzo-soprano); Mandryka, a rich Croatian landowner (baritone); Matteo, a poor officer (tenor); Count Elemer, one of Arabella's suitors (tenor); the Fiakermilli, "mascot" of the Coachmen's Ball (coloratura soprano)

Scoring: piccolo, 3 flutes, 2 oboes, English horn, 3 clarinets, bass clarinet, 3 bassoons, contrabassoon, 4 horns, 3 trumpets, 3 trombones, tuba, harp, sleigh bells, tambourine, bass drum, cymbals, timpani, strings

This last observation also applies to Strauss' next homage to Vienna. *Arabella* is an opera about a glass of water. Well, not exactly, but it might as well be, in the sense that it remains a problematic piece. A lyric comedy, it has suffered from bad karma in a few ways. First, Strauss' favorite librettist, Hugo von Hofmannsthal, died without quite finalizing the libretto. For years it was believed that Strauss, true to his word, set the text as he received it without changing a word. Recent scholarship has since proved this not to be the case, but it might still be argued that Strauss' reverence for his late colleague's work compelled him to set just a few too many of Hofmannsthal's words—all two and a half hours of them.

Second, taken purely as comedy, the opera has its witty bits but in general isn't very amusing. As you will see, the situations either are not outrageous enough, or come across merely as silly. This doesn't mean the opera can't be staged in a truly humorous way, but it doesn't seem to have been, and it's almost never discussed in comedic terms. The story comes across as a collection of situations and characters that Strauss has done better elsewhere. Arabella herself has a certain unassailable dignity. Although her situation is quite different—she is the unmarried oldest child of a noble family that is down on its luck—her poise and self-awareness sometimes recall that of the Marschallin.

The Fiakermilli, the rather annoying female "mascot" of the Vienna Coachmen's Ball, recalls *Ariadne*'s Zerbinetta, coloratura and all, only without the latter's relevance to the plot and with no real aria. The ball was a yearly Viennese event that appealed to Strauss on account of its local color; ultimately, it became superfluous as a plot device, and the Fiakermilli even more so. Arabella's sister, Zdenka, spends much of the opera dressed as a guy named Zdenko, for reasons we'll discuss later, but Strauss and Hofmannsthal do little to exploit the humorous possibilities of her situation even though her role in the unfolding story is an important one.

Here is the scenario, then, which takes place in a Viennese hotel, circa 1860: Arabella wants to marry for love; her parents, who are broke, want her to marry for money. Because they can't afford to subsidize the "coming out" in society of two girls, Zdenka, their younger daughter and a really good sport, runs around disguised as a teenage boy. Zdenka is in love with Matteo, a poor nobody, who actually loves Arabella. In order to keep Matteo around, Zdenka has been sending him love letters purportedly signed by Arabella. In act 1, Arabella sings an absolutely gorgeous aria, later a duet with Zdenka, that says, effectively, "I'll know the guy who's right for me when I see him." In fact, she thinks she *has* seen him, in the form of a mysterious stranger out on the street.

Meanwhile, Arabella's father laments his inability to hit up his old army buddies for cash. Even the super-wealthy Croatian Mandryka has not answered his letters, despite his having included a picture of Arabella as an incentive (kind of distasteful, isn't it?). Also, three different noble gentlemen have been courting Arabella without success, the most important of whom is Elemer, the tenor lead. Although he gets a vocally rewarding scene with Arabella after her "Mr. Right" aria in the first act, there is curiously little tension between them, or between Elemer and the various other suitors. It's all very nice, almost genteel.

A visitor soon appears to meet Arabella's father, announcing himself as Mandryka, only it's the nephew of the older Mandryka, who is actually dead. The nephew Mandryka is his uncle's heir, has lots of money, and has seen Arabella's picture and fallen madly in love. He asks to marry her and gives Arabella's father some much-needed cash. When they meet during the second-act ball, Arabella realizes that Mandryka is the mysterious stranger she has seen on the street and has been waiting for, and she accepts his offer of marriage.

So everything should be fine *except* that Zdenka, disguised as Arabella's brother Zdenko, slips Matteo an envelope containing what purports to be the key to Arabella's hotel room (obviously, it is Zdenka's). Mandryka gets wind of it and is furious. The usual complications ensue, but it all gets sorted out in the end. Arabella's parents get the money, and both she and Zdenka get their respective guys. Perhaps the funniest moment in the opera is the orchestral interlude at the start of act 3, which features Strauss in his most frantically exuberant sex-music mode as he wordlessly depicts Zdenka and Matteo's passionate assignation. Because they do it in the dark, Matteo thinks he has made love to Arabella, hence the above-mentioned complications.

Oh, yes, that glass of water. Mandryka tells Arabella that in his country, it is the custom for a woman to accept a man's proposal of marriage by presenting him with a glass of water. So Arabella gives him one at the end of the opera. Comparisons to the presentation of the silver rose in *Der Rosenkavalier* are superficially obvious and not terribly relevant. Nevertheless, they are not to *Arabella*'s advantage either dramatically or musically, although the brief final duet is stunning. The glass of water is not a bad idea—rather sweet, really—but you can't help having that "been there, heard that" feeling if you know Strauss' earlier opera at all well, just as the effort to marry off Arabella to the highest bidder works more convincingly in the mythological context of *Danae*.

Although very Viennese in flavor, with ubiquitous waltz rhythms, *Arabella* also deserves to be categorized with Strauss' other domestic comedies. The characters are all regular people, at least of the period. There is no magic, nothing mythical, and very little of the sheer glamour of *Der Rosenkavalier*, or even *Schlagobers*. By Strauss' own standards, the instrumentation is quite plain: the exact number of strings is not specified, which means that they won't be as frequently subdivided into multiple parts as in his other scores. Extra percussion appears only in act 1: the sleigh bells are part of the action, while the bass drum, cymbals, and tambourine play just a few soft notes within the same couple of bars. You could leave them out and probably never notice the difference. There is no stage band either, despite the ball scene in act 2.

That said, the orchestration is as sensitively handled as it was in *Helena*, always supporting and never covering the voices. Aside from the glorious writing for Arabella herself, Mandryka's music is also very characterful, particularly his entrance aria, which has almost the bounce and melodic appeal of one of Dvořák's *Slavonic Dances*. The duet between the two lovers when they meet at the ball also sounds memorably romantic, and the two Zdenka/Arabella duets reveal Strauss' unsurpassed lyrical effulgence when writing for multiple soprano voices. Even if the overall story is not especially funny, Strauss' mastery of conversational pacing can be heard to great advantage later in act 2, where some actual spoken dialogue interrupts the music at several points without ever seeming to halt its onward flow.

I need to be clear about one point: when I say Strauss' orchestration in this opera is "plain," I am speaking purely relatively. Even at his plainest, Strauss is positively gaudy next to, say, Brahms. The ordinariness of the instrumentation matches that of the characters themselves. It creates its own ambience and suits the setting.

Ultimately, *Arabella* is the prima donna's opera. For years it was practically the personal property of the iconic Strauss soprano Lisa Della Casa (1919–2012), and without a great Arabella the piece cannot hope to succeed. However, opera as an art form is special in that stellar singing forgives any number of sins with respect to the dramatic plausibility of the storyline. The important thing is that the composer gives the soloists enough wonderful music to justify the audience's time and attention. For all the work's flaws, many of which are in any case a matter of personal opinion, Strauss certainly does that.

Capriccio (1942)

Major Characters: The Countess (soprano); Flamand, a composer (tenor); Olivier, a poet (baritone); Clairon, an actress (contralto); the Count, brother of the Countess (baritone); La Roche, a theater director (bass)

Scoring: piccolo, 3 flutes, 2 oboes, English horn, 3 clarinets, basset horn, bass clarinet, 3 bassoons, contrabassoon, 4 horns, 2 trumpets, 3 trombones, cymbals, bass drum, 2 harps, harpsichord, 16 first and 16 second violins, 10 violas, 10 cellos, 6 basses

Onstage: string sextet, violin, cello, harpsichord

Strauss' last tribute to Enlightenment Europe, *Capriccio*, was also his last opera altogether. To understand how far he had come since his first great theatrical success, *Salome*, consider the interesting fact that both operas conclude with a fifteen-minute-long solo *scena* for the lead soprano, followed by a one-line "coda" of commentary by a major male character. In *Salome*, that line is "Someone kill that woman!" In *Capriccio*, it is "Madame, supper is served." However, the best explanation of what Strauss was about in this last opera can be found in the lengthy preface appended to the full score (Verlag Dr. Richard Strauss, 1996; tr. Stewart Spencer):

> The patron saint of this theatrical comedy, the idea of which was first suggested by the title of a forgotten libretto [set by Salieri] by the Abbé de Casti, *Primo le parole, dopo la musica (First the Words, Then the Music)*, is Gluck, who reformed the whole style of composition and whose preface to *Alceste* determined the course of music drama for an entire century. I hope that I myself, standing at the end of this development, may be allowed, after 50 years of

experience as a conductor, to add a brief epilogue on the subject of reforming current performing practice and offer advice that may be of use, particularly in the context of *Capriccio*, to those of my esteemed colleagues who take upon themselves the by no means thankless task of giving serious study to my operatic scores.

Strauss proceeds to give a series of tips on how to conduct rehearsals, then theorizes on the relationship of the voice to the orchestra throughout operatic history, from Mozart through Verdi and Wagner. This preface is not without a certain degree of condescension, even chutzpah, and it clearly reveals just how highly our "first-class second-rate composer" thought of himself and his output. But more importantly, it reveals how seriously Strauss took his position in the great line of operatic reformers starting with Gluck and continuing through Wagner. German opera composers, it seems, are sort of like the Japanese with cars and consumer electronics: they may not have invented them, but they improved the basic concept.

The setting of *Capriccio* is quite specific as to period and locale: a chateau just outside of Paris, "at the time when Gluck was beginning his operatic reforms, around 1775." Actually, Gluck's operatic reforms had begun in Vienna in the early 1760s, but neither they (nor he) reached Paris until a decade later. The references to Gluck are ironic. He was concerned with restoring dramatic logic and naturalness of pacing to the operatic stage. *Capriccio* is more like an episode of *Seinfeld*. Dramatically speaking, it is an opera about nothing, "a conversation piece," as Strauss subtitled it, concerning the relative importance of words and music.

The characters are archetypes. Two idealistic artists, one a composer, the other a poet, vie for the love of the Countess Madeleine. The theater director, La Roche, as well as the actress Clairon, deflate their lofty idealism. The Countess' brother, who believes that opera in general is silly, pursues Clairon. The poet writes a sonnet for the Countess, which the composer sets to music. They have an argument about the reforms of Gluck, whom the Countess supports, and sing a vocal fugue on the subject of music versus words. Two Italian singers show up at the behest of La Roche and behave as a disdainful German composer in

1942 might believe that Italian singers would: the tenor worries about being paid, and the soprano eats too much and gets drunk.

Composer and poet agree to write an opera about their aesthetic dispute, and the Countess must determine the outcome, and thus the ending of the opera, the next morning. She is left alone with her thoughts, and *Capriccio* closes with her going in to supper, undecided as to how the story must end, although she's clearly leaning toward music. Her choice has personal implications: the winner, Strauss suggests, will also become her lover. The warmth of Strauss' score and the wittiness of the text quite wonderfully humanize a debate that risks looking hopelessly arid when described on paper.

With its unusually large string section and deliciously anachronistic harpsichord, *Capriccio* is a compendium of techniques for text setting, including spoken dialogue, accompanied recitative, large-scale ensembles, arias, and duets, and concluding with one of Strauss' very greatest solo scenes for the soprano voice. The work's single act plays for a bit more than two and a quarter hours, not long at all by operatic standards, though many performances divide the piece in half in actual performance to give the audience a break and allow the theater to open the bar during intermission. Strauss very cleverly increases the musical tension throughout, placing much of the recitation and dialogue toward the beginning, gradually working up to the more musically ambitious ensembles and, of course, the great closing scene, which is preceded by the only purely instrumental music in the entire work since the opening string sextet—the "Moonlight Music" interlude, with its glorious horn solo. Music gradually takes over and tells us far more about how the story will end than the libretto itself ever does.

The circumstances of *Capriccio*'s 1942 premiere were, in hindsight, surreal. World War II and its attendant atrocities were at their height. Joseph Goebbels, who hated Strauss personally, sponsored the production. It was only due to the political savvy of librettist and conductor Clemens Krauss that the work was performed at all. Strauss never intended that *Capriccio*, a true connoisseur's piece, should be popular, but then he never counted on the power of recordings. EMI's premiere release from the mid-1950s, featuring soprano Elisabeth Schwarzkopf and conductor Wolfgang Sawallisch, permitted listeners to enjoy a work that few would ever get to see staged. Several other recordings have since followed, featuring major Strauss sopranos such as Gundula Janowitz and Kiri Te Kanawa in the role of the Countess, and the work gradually has come to be recognized as a masterpiece by many Strauss aficionados despite enjoying relatively few productions.

Capriccio succeeds on account of its complete honesty. It truly is "a conversation piece" and never pretends otherwise. It moves at a realistic pace, considering with both wit and grace a topic that obviously meant a great deal to Strauss. Although set in a stylized and mythological "Enlightenment Europe," the music is not so much retrospective or nostalgic as it is a celebration and summary of a century and a half of operatic development. Strauss was not wrong in describing himself, in *Capriccio*'s preface, as "standing at the end" of this great period of artist achievement.

What can seem disconcerting about *Capriccio*, and late Strauss in general, is that we as listeners are taught to look at musical history as a succession of idiomatically distinct, often aesthetically hostile periods. The elaborately ornamental baroque style was succeeded by the simple purity and proportion of the classical period, followed in turn by the hot-and-heavy romantics, who were spurned by the neoclassicists and the rise of atonality. Strauss, on the other hand, saw the entire process whole, as a continuous development of a single tradition, and his late music expresses this unity. Sometimes it sounds conservative, sometimes radical, but in reality it looks neither backward nor forward, but broadly, at the big picture. That is the vision expounded in *Capriccio*, and the further we get from the twentieth century, the more clear and correct it seems.

Exoticism and Eroticism
Salome, Josephs Legende, and Die Frau ohne Schatten

f you're looking for lavish, luscious, late-romantic musical excess, then these three works go about as far as possible in that direction. Others came later—the operas of Schreker, Zemlinsky, Korngold, and even late Puccini, not to mention extravaganzas such as Schoenberg's *Gurre-Lieder*—but Strauss was the first, and remains arguably the best, exponent of this particular aesthetic niche. The taste for exotic subjects was not so much German as French: think of such works as Delibes' *Lakmé*, Massenet's *Thaïs*, or Saint-Saëns' *Samson and Delilah*, further fortified by the orchestral and operatic essays of Russian composers such as Rimsky-Korsakov (*Antar, Scheherazade, Sadko, The Tale of Tsar Saltan*) and his school.

Salome (1905)

Major Characters: Salome (soprano); Jochanaan (John the Baptist) (baritone); Narraboth, captain of the guard (tenor); a page (alto); Herodes (Herod), Tetrarch of Judaea and Perea (tenor); Herodias, his wife (mezzo-soprano)

Scoring: piccolo, 3 flutes, 2 oboes, English horn, heckelphone, 5 clarinets, bass clarinet, 3 bassoons, contrabassoon, 6 horns, 4 trumpets, 4 trombones, tuba, tam-tam, cymbals, bass drum, snare drum, tambourine, triangle, xylophone, glockenspiel, castanets, timpani (2 players), 2 harps, celesta, organ, harmonium, 16 first and 16 second violins, 10–12 violas, 10 cellos, 8 basses

What Strauss and the Germans brought to the exotic party was sex, thanks mainly to Wagner's steamy *Tristan und Isolde*, with or without that opera's heavy-duty philosophical subtext. Strauss' first major operatic excursion into this erotic-cum-exotic fantasyland was his setting of Oscar Wilde's French-language play *Salomé*. Like the tone poem *Also sprach Zarathustra*, which it actually resembles in many ways, the work takes as its starting point a very Wagnerian method and technique but places it in service of a wholly un-Wagnerian subject. Salome's closing scene, in which she sings with orgasmic passion to the severed head of John the Baptist before kissing it on the lips, is a sort of anti-*Liebestod*, a perverse parody of Isolde's death scene.

In this, as in so many other ways, *Salome* is a very disturbing opera, a fact that we are likely to forget—first, because the music is so gorgeous and so familiar, and second, because culturally we have become desensitized to scenes of appalling violence and depravity. Strauss forces us to confront frightening ugliness by presenting it in the guise of innocence and beauty. The result is literally a guilty pleasure. An early performer of the title role once asked Strauss how she should handle the challenge of acting out Salome's demented sexual obsession, and Strauss reportedly told her, "Don't worry about it. The music is already disgusting enough." Nevertheless, when you get a singing actress like Catherine Malfitano, for example, whose tormented lust practically oozes from her pores in her stunning video performance, it's possible to recapture something of the shock and horror that that the work inflicted on its original audiences.

Salome has been described as a tone poem with voices, which is very close to the truth. The story is beyond terse: Salome is the daughter of Herodias and Herod's brother, Herod II. Both Herods are sons of Herod the Great, but from different mothers. Therefore, the Herod of the opera (actually known historically as Herod Antipas) is Salome's uncle, which does not stop him from lusting after her shamefully to her mother's—that is, Herod's wife's—growing disgust. Salome in turn develops a licentious passion for John the Baptist (Jochanaan), and when he rejects her and gets sent back to the cistern in which he is being kept, she gets Herod to promise her anything she wants if she will dance for him. He agrees; she performs "The Dance of the Seven Veils," ending naked before him. Salome requests as a reward the head of Jochanaan. She gets it, sings a revolting "love scene" with it, and kisses it, and in repugnance Herod orders his soldiers to crush her to death beneath their shields. Much like *Elektra*, it's all over in about an hour and forty minutes.

Wilde's play has a sort of built-in musical structure that adapts perfectly to a musical setting. For example, Salome's role essentially consists of three duets, each with three sections, then her final solo scene. First she asks the guard captain Narraboth, who is in love with her, three times to permit her to speak to Jochanaan. Then she attempts to seduce Jochanaan three times, saying she desires his body, then his hair, and then his mouth. Finally, after her dance, Herod attempts three times to dissuade her from claiming her reward, promising her three alternative gifts. So the number three figures prominently in the music as a structural principle. To this arrangement Strauss adds a system of *Zarathustra*-like Leitmotivs: the twitchy, three- or four-note motive of Salome's madness that reappears, upside down, at the start of *Elektra*; the very opening figure on the clarinet that represents Salome; Jochanaan's somewhat off-kilter brass tunes (Strauss called the character "a clown"); and others that you can hear clearly as the work proceeds.

Salome's famous dance (CD Track 4) has long been a popular concert showpiece, but with its snake-charmer oboes and "tempo di hoochy-koochy" rhythms—to use Stravinsky's memorable phrase—never mind the accompaniment derived from Salome's repeated demand for Jochanaan's head, it has also been derided critically as kitsch. To my way of thinking, that is just what Strauss was after. *Salome* features possibly the four most loathsome characters in all of opera; to accuse Strauss' music for them of being in bad taste is to miss the point. They are indisputably low-class. Herod is a lecherous weasel, Herodias a vindictive shrew. Salome we already know about, and Jochanaan's relentless piety is akin to hectoring. Indeed, he is if anything even more psychotically fanatical than is Salome, and Strauss makes no secret of his dislike of the character. Their encounters constitute a study in two opposing brands of obsession, the religious versus the sexual, and if the sexual wins this time around, Strauss seems to say, that's just too bad. Neither is better than the other.

This is an important point, and a recurring theme with Strauss, who disliked any form of religious expression. In a medium full of prayers, church scenes, and the musical opportunities that they afford, it is very telling that Strauss' operas after *Guntram* contain virtually nothing of spiritual or religious significance. Some commentators have tried to find in Salome a tinge of anti-Semitism in Strauss' handling of the constantly quarreling Jews—the opera's only truly comic moment. Musically it is a very funny contrapuntal mishmash, and aside from a few remarks about how Herod (and everyone else) finds the Jews' endless religious squabbling tiresome, there is nothing uniquely offensive about Strauss' handling of these minor characters. Salome herself says that she *really* hates the Romans, and Strauss' Jewish vignette doesn't hold a candle to what he has in store for Jochanaan.

When the guard captain Narraboth kills himself and falls dead between Salome and Jochanaan, *neither* of them even notices. They are both far too lost in their own narcissism to care about it one bit. Jochanaan, when he's not speaking cryptically about Jesus, spends most of his time cursing at Herodias in the most obnoxious and vividly offensive terms. That she may well deserve it is beside the point; he is wholly intolerant and the very opposite of a benign, saintly, theoretically religious personality. Not the least of the objections to this opera in the years following the premiere—once we get past the scandalous "Dance of the Seven Veils"—stemmed from this unflattering portrayal of the religious figure of Jochanaan, yet another aspect of the music's anti-Wagnerian philosophical stance. Cosima Wagner condemned it roundly.

Salome's final scene (CD Track 5) features some of Strauss' very best sex music. At its climax, when she kisses the severed head, the orchestra screams with a dissonant chord very similar to the equally dissonant climax of the love scene in the *Symphonia Domestica*. An intense sexual climax can toy with the boundaries between pleasure and pain, and as we all know, there are people who find it difficult if not impossible to distinguish between the two. But this scene is much more than that; it also acts as a recapitulation of all the main themes and motives in the opera.

For example, just after five minutes in both the "Dance of the Seven Veils" and Salome's solo, you will hear exactly the same music, only the words now give meaning to her previous dance: "Nothing in the world was so white as your body; nothing in the world was as dark as your hair; in the whole world there was nothing as red as your mouth," she sings. Herod's horrified reaction to Herodias ("She is monstrous, your daughter") and specifically his cry that "Something terrible will happen," uttered just before Salome's final apotheosis, repeats the page's warning to Narraboth from the opera's start. Events have come full circle.

Strauss' orchestral invention throughout the opera generally achieves a level of graphic specificity that really has to be heard to be believed, whether in its explicit eroticism, the illustration of Herod's auditory hallucinations, the unforgettable "sound of silence" as Salome waits for the executioner to carry out Jochanaan's death sentence, the high trill and twitchy motive of her madness, or the moment when Jochanaan's head appears (the start of CD Track 5) and the orchestra reacts with as terrifying an evocation of absolute evil and terror as any film score you would care to mention.

With *Salome*, Strauss "arrived" as an opera composer. The work created a scandalous sensation of the best kind. It was banned in Vienna despite everything Gustav Mahler tried to do to get it past the censors there. It survived one performance in New York in 1907 before being booted off the stage of the Metropolitan Opera (allegedly by popular request) for nearly three decades, and in London the libretto had to be modified to remove any possible offensive references to Jochanaan, who became simply "the prophet." All of this only increased the public's appetite to see what all the fuss was about. In 1930, Strauss arranged a French-language version using Wilde's original text, and it has been recorded for those who prefer French to German. Strauss later boasted that the royalties from *Salome* paid for his house in Garmisch.

Finally, a world about the title role itself: Salome is Strauss' first great homage to the soprano voice. The part requires a singer with the vocal stamina and heft of a dramatic soprano, the body of a young girl, and the athleticism of a ballerina who doesn't mind ripping her clothes off at the end of her dance. She works hard from the moment she comes onstage at the start of the opera, never leaves for any significant period of time, and needs to save the best for last. Finding all of these qualities in a single person has proven very difficult over the years. Opera does tend to be forgiving of physical imperfection when the voice is magnificent, and so many singers have assayed the role without really looking the part. It's a perennial problem, but it is also a tribute to Strauss' gripping musical setting that it hasn't prevented the work from becoming a repertory staple.

Josephs Legende (1914)

Scoring: 2 piccolos, 4 flutes, 3 oboes, English horn, heckelphone, 3 clarinets, bass clarinet, contrabass clarinet, 4 bassoons, contrabassoon, 6 horns, 4 trumpets, 4 trombones, tenor tuba, bass tuba, glockenspiel, xylophone, triangle, tambourine, cymbals, bass drum, snare drum, castanets, 2 small cymbals, tam-tam, wind machine, 4 harps, piano, organ, celesta, 10 first, 10 second, and 10 third violins, 8 first and 8 second violas, 6 first and 6 second cellos, 8 basses

Strauss' next foray into musical exoticism also involved a biblical subject. *Josephs Legende* was commissioned by Diaghilev for his Ballets Russes. It was a very prestigious opportunity. No other major German composer received a commission from the Paris-based organization, and Strauss was understandably concerned that the work should be a success. As it turned out, although by no means a failure, *Josephs Legende* had a bumpy ride, and commentators until very recently have been looking for opportunities to trash the piece. As with so many other lesser-known Strauss works, recordings have played a major role in rehabilitating the music's reputation, but this only begs the question as to how it got a bad rap in the first place.

The problems began with Strauss himself. He had issues with the scenario, which was by Hofmannsthal and Count Harry Kessler, finding the character of Joseph boring because he's sweet and innocent and God-seeking. Strauss said as much, and his disparaging of the main character always gets quoted in the literature about the piece. And he was right. Joseph *is* boring. Most one-dimensional, sweet, and chaste characters are, nowhere more so than in a ballet, but all that means is that Strauss had to work harder to make him musically interesting. He certainly had no problem with Barak in *Die Frau ohne Schatten*, who is if anything even more saintly with far less excuse.

Then, evidently, Kessler and Hofmannsthal had the idea of adding some kind of mystical or philosophical symbolism to the story that makes even less sense in a ballet, where no one says anything, than it does in an opera, where they can at least sing about it. Dance is perfectly helpless to convey anything more complicated than basic emotions of good or bad, happy or sad, or whatever may be suggested in pantomime by facial expression, body language, movement, or gesture, and Strauss was well aware of it.

However, the scenario as it stands seems to have come close to what Strauss wanted. Potiphar's wife sits bored at one of her husband's parties. Nothing interests her until Joseph shows up. She attempts to seduce him, but he rejects her, so she arranges that her husband will catch the two of them together, at which time she can take the revenge of a woman scorned. Suddenly the angel of Joseph's dream shows up and rescues him, and Potiphar's wife strangles herself with her own strand of pearls. Joseph and the angel march out together into the light (evidently all that's left of the philosophical part).

This being a ballet, there are large chunks in which neither Joseph nor Potiphar's wife figure at all: the women's Wedding Dance, the Dance of the Boxers, Dance of the Slave Girls—that sort of thing. The dance for the men, with its exotic timpani ostinato, recalls the famous bacchanal from *Samson and Delilah* by Saint-Saëns, a composer whom Strauss admired in his youth. For Joseph, who features in only about half of the work, Strauss came up with a lovely sonority based on high woodwinds, harps, celesta, and piano, tinged with the neoclassicism recently acquired in *Le bourgeois gentilhomme* and *Ariadne*. This is a clever touch: the youth and purity of the character recall the music of a more "innocent" age.

The truth is that Strauss had no trouble portraying innocence and chastity in, say, *Daphne* or *Danae*, and he has no issue with it here. Whether he liked doing it or not really is beside the point. The music representing Joseph is perfectly fine as it stands. Potiphar's wife, of course, offers plenty of opportunity for the sort of juicy stuff that Strauss loved, and the episodes of temptation, along with the final scene of Joseph's getting framed and then rescued, are wonderful and more than appropriately climactic. This last bit, with its imaginative use of the wind machine and other cool orchestral effects, foreshadows the similar temptation scenes in *Die Frau ohne Schatten*, Strauss' very next work.

So in order to sustain the myth that Strauss hated the scenario and therefore wrote bad music, we would have to believe, first, that his favorite librettist didn't know or care about his strengths as a composer and deliberately tried to sabotage him with a scenario he hated, and second, that Strauss had neither the ability nor the desire to succeed in writing a major commission for a Paris premiere at the Ballets Russes, to be danced by ballet superstar Vaslav Nijinsky, no less. Does either of these two possibilities sound reasonable?

As it turned out, Nijinsky suddenly decided to get married shortly before the premiere, which was odd because he was very gay, and his boyfriend happened to be Diaghilev. The shocked and presumably heartbroken Diaghilev fired him immediately, leaving the premiere to the exceptionally talented but at this time still inexperienced Léonide Massine. Then World War I broke out a few weeks after the premiere. This one-two punch put the kibosh on any chance the work had to establish itself in the repertoire or even to get a fair hearing by enough people to gain a good impression of its strengths and weaknesses. It just fell off the radar, and everyone assumed that it was junk on the basis of Strauss' biographical grumbling. Strauss made a concert suite for reduced orchestra from *Josephs Legende* very late in his life, long after he had moved on to more important things.

So much for why the work has been unfairly judged by posterity; the question remains: Is it good music? Well, both yes and no. Regarded more as a tone poem than a ballet, it can certainly hold its own, and that really is how it deserves to be judged. No one has seriously claimed that the work is poorly constructed, and assessing the quality of its thematic invention remains very much a matter of personal taste. Those who condemned it at the time of its premiere had yet to come to grips with Strauss' new, neoclassical style, and some viewed those elements, mistakenly, as a sign of flagging inspiration.

As a ballet, though, I can see how the music could be problematic. Nijinsky considered it to be undanceable, but then the Bolshoi said the same about Prokofiev's *Romeo and Juliet*, so comments like that don't carry much weight. They come with the territory. Instrumental soloists also love to kvetch that such-and-such composer didn't really understand "their" instrument when writing a concerto for it. There is nonetheless a very real incompatibility between Strauss' mature style and the conventions of ballet music, and this has to do with questions of rhythm.

Dance music by definition has to be very rhythmic—whether complex and syncopated, as in Stravinsky's *The Rite of Spring*, or more conventionally straightforward. Strauss obviously had no problem writing simple dances, such as waltzes or minuets. His works are full of them. However, his more symphonic music depends for much of its fluidity on intricate divisions of the beat within the bar, concealing what is often a fairly simple larger-scale phrase rhythm. What this means is that the music retains traditional four- and eight-bar periods but often doesn't sound like it because of its elaborate inner detail, displaced accents, and lack of literal repetition. In this he resembles Wagner, who similarly avoided simple, repetitive rhythms in order to create his characteristic "endless melody." This is not a good recipe for a successful ballet.

Strauss was certainly aware of this problem. Indeed, he largely solved it in *Schlagobers*; but here, his resort to traditional percussive effects such as lots of soft cymbal crashes or tambourine rolls to help mark the time tends to weigh the music down, even though the score is peppered with injunctions to push the tempo along and speed up successively. It's a subtle but noticeable issue, one that may bother some listeners more than others. When Strauss is being Strauss, he's perfectly fine. When he tries to write ballet music, he sometimes sounds uncharacteristically forced. Fortunately, there is an easy solution to this problem if only conductors would take it: keep the music moving swiftly forward. Ideally the work should run for under an hour; over that, and there's a greater risk of encountering dead spots. The best performances, on disc at least, proceed accordingly.

There is certainly no shame in any of this. The ballet repertoire is full of works that succeed far better in concert than they do onstage, Stravinsky's aforementioned *The Rite of Spring* among them. The same holds true for Debussy's *Prelude to the Afternoon of a Faun* and Ravel's *Boléro*, to name just two others. If *Josephs Legende* has been enjoying a renaissance as of late, it is entirely due to the fact that it makes for very enjoyable listening as a concert piece, or at home on recordings. Failure in one format does not preclude success in others, whatever the composer's initial intentions may have been.

Die Frau ohne Schatten (The Woman Without a Shadow) (1919)

Major Characters: The Empress (soprano); the Emperor (tenor); the Nurse (mezzo-soprano); Barak the Dyer (baritone); the Dyer's Wife (soprano)

Scoring: 2 piccolos, 4 flutes, 3 oboes, English horn, 4 clarinets, bass clarinet, 4 bassoons, contrabassoon, 8 horns, 4 tenor tubas, 4 trumpets, 4 trombones, tuba, glockenspiel, xylophone, 5 Chinese gongs, cymbals, snare drum, rute (twig brush), sleigh bells, bass drum, large tenor drum, triangle, tambourine, castanets, tam-tam, glass harmonica (tuned water glasses), 2 celestas, 2 harps, 16 first and 16 second violins, 6 first, 6 second, and 6 third violas, 6 first and 6 second cellos, 8 basses

Stage band: 2 flutes, oboe, 2 clarinets, bassoon, horn, 6 trumpets, 6 trombones, wind machine, thunder machine, organ, 4 tam-tams

If the timing of *Josephs Legende*—and *Schlagobers*, for that matter—may have been poor, the same holds true for *Die Frau ohne Schatten*. It premiered in 1919 and is now considered by many to be Strauss' greatest opera, but a devastated Germany was in no mood for a grandiose, lavish, expensive extravaganza vaguely modeled on Mozart's *The Magic Flute* in which two couples, one aristocratic and one lowborn, learn about the joys of marriage and childbearing. Strauss always had faith in the work, with good reason, but came to call it by the acronym *FROSCH*, which means "frog" in German, on account of its hapless fortunes.

The fact is that by this time in his career, Strauss truly believed he had done enough to have earned the freedom to write whatever he wanted, and that in return for his contributions to national culture, Germany owed him the courtesy of spending a fortune to produce the result. He never accepted that the end of the aristocracy also spelled the end of the almost limitless patronage of the arts that he had enjoyed in the period prior to World War I. The Kaiser was gone, and so were the days, in Europe at least, when art would remain the personal hobby of the incredibly wealthy, financed on the backs of the working classes. Henceforth, both politics and the tyranny of the box office would hold sway, and Strauss was obliged to adapt to the new reality as best he could. As events would prove, he never really did.

Never mind. *Frau* is an amazing score, composed with a virtuosity and polish astonishing even when compared to *Salome* and *Elektra*. Strauss really pulled out all the stops for this one. It has great tunes, startling orchestral sonorities from a massive ensemble, and that curious simplicity of many of its motives—a kind of innocence almost— that appears in Strauss' work beginning with *An Alpine Symphony*. It is addictive. It's also amazingly coherent given both the weirdness of the story and its three-hour-plus length. For that weirdness we have Hofmannsthal to thank, once again, and although there's a lot of serious symbolism to take in, once we accept a couple of basic premises the plot turns out to be a lot less contrived than, say, that for *Helena*. It simply operates according to those irrational and arbitrary rules that bring all fantasies or fairy tales to life. So here we go.

The story takes place in the mythical "Southeastern Islands." Keikobad, whom we never meet, is the ruler of the spirit realm. He has a shape-shifting daughter who, while in the form of a gazelle, tangles with the Emperor's favorite hunting falcon one day. As the Emperor captures her, she loses her magic shape-shifting talisman and turns into a beautiful woman. They fall in love, and the Emperor makes her his Empress. Evidently they inhabit a region midway between the spirit realm and grubby old planet earth, but this isn't entirely clear and doesn't especially matter.

However, unbeknownst to the Emperor, her talisman also contains a curse: once he has claimed the Empress, he has one year to get her pregnant or he will be turned to stone and she will be whisked back to her father's realm. And although he's been trying enthusiastically to do his part on a nightly basis, there's another problem he doesn't know about: she casts no shadow, and therefore can't get pregnant. Never mind why. Those are the rules. When the opera opens, she's got three days either to acquire a shadow by hook or by crook, or find herself married to an Emperor-shaped chunk of granite.

The Empress is accompanied by her Nurse, a nasty old witch who hates mortals and isn't too keen on the Emperor either. She works for Keikobad and has the job of keeping tabs on the Empress. The role of the Nurse is one of the great operatic challenges for mezzo-soprano: the vocal writing is as wild as that for Klytaemnestra, but a lot longer and both higher and lower. She tells the Empress that she has a way of obtaining a shadow for her, but it involves a very unpleasant trip down to the world of men. The Empress agrees to make the journey, and away they go, to the sounds of an incredibly extravagant orchestral interlude that makes Wagner's descent into Nibelheim in *Das Rheingold* sound like a trip to the corner convenience store.

Throughout the opera, Strauss takes great pains to characterize the three main realms: Keikobad's features ominous chorales in the low brass with heavy percussion, while the Emperor and Empress are accompanied by strings, horns, harps, and (for the falcon) chirping woodwinds. Barak the Dyer's home/workshop sounds like one—muted brass plus the dry, percussive noises of rute, castanets, xylophone, and tuned gongs play simple, repetitive rhythms suggestive of industrial activity. You can hear plainly how the orchestra illustrates the Empress' journey by marking the clear transition from the instrumentation of her realm to Barak's.

The Empress and the Nurse finally arrive at the home of Barak and his wife, who is simply called "the Dyer's Wife." Barak is the only character in the whole story with a name, aside from Keikobad, who is nothing *but* a name—plus the dark, gnarly three-note Leitmotiv with which the opera begins and that looms menacingly over the entire work. Barak also has three brothers who have, respectively, one eye, one arm, and a hunchback. They come straight from the world of Grimm's fairy tales but otherwise have little to do with the plot. They represent the sad lives of those who live by toil and the unhappy lot of mankind more generally.

The Dyer's Wife, on the other hand, is the most interesting character in the opera. Modeled on Strauss' wife Pauline, whom Hofmannsthal never liked, she is a shrew with a good heart. Her fears and insecurities take the form of a sharp tongue that hides her basic decency and need for love. Barak, in contrast, is an incredibly hardworking saint who can't understand why she won't lighten up and "give him children," as the saying goes. Disgusted with her situation, she appears ripe to be taken advantage of by some shadow-snatching magic Nurse and her mysterious companion.

The Nurse promises Barak's wife jewels and the love of a hunky stranger in a tacky harem costume if she renounces the possibility of pregnancy and thus gives up her shadow, an idea close to Wagner's Alberich renouncing love in order to forge the ring that will make him master of the universe; but as always with Strauss, the difference humanizes the concept. The Nurse and the Empress will remain with the Dyer's Wife as servants for three days, after which time she must make up her mind to forfeit the shadow. Barak, unable to understand what has come over his wife, reminisces nostalgically about his hopes and disappointments while the neighborhood watch brings the first act to a close by singing beautifully but for rather too long about the joys of connubial bliss.

Act 2 is brilliantly put together in a very clear sort of rondo form: ABACA. This is not only musically satisfying; it also encourages some visually spectacular scene changes. Its sections are:

A: Barak's house
B: The Emperor's solo scene
A: Barak's house
C: The Empress' solo scene (and dream sequence)
A: Barak's house

In the Emperor's scene, which is introduced by a marvelously vocal cello solo, he spends a lot of time talking to his falcon, which he has been looking for ever since he sent it away for attacking the gazelle that later became the Empress. He has also spotted his wife slinking mysteriously around his hunting lodge and smelled the stench of mortal men on her. He believes she is being unfaithful and resolves to kill her; then he changes his mind and decides to run away and feel sorry for himself.

The Empress, meanwhile, in her solo scene has a lot to feel guilty about. She dreams of her husband entering Keikobad's realm (thrilling, phantasmagoric orchestration) and bemoans the fact that he does not know of the curse that is about to descend on him. She also is touched by Barak's kindness and saddened by his hard life. Humans, it seems, aren't as bad as she has been led to believe, and she is having second thoughts about taking the wife's shadow. In short, she's a mess, but as always with Strauss' writing for soprano, it's a vocally glorious mess.

Down below, things are also going from bad to worse at Barak's place. Initially he has a great day at the market and brings back a crowd to celebrate, but his wife freaks out even as they ignore her and sing a very catchy chorus. In their next scene, the nurse gives him a sleeping potion so she can continue to tempt his wife, but Mrs. Barak gets even more upset, wakes him up to berate him, and runs out of the house. Finally, in the third scene, all hell breaks loose. Barak's wife renounces childbearing and loses her shadow. The Empress says she sees blood on it and will not take it despite the Nurse's urgings. Pity the shadow, caught between the two squabbling women. A sword appears in Barak's hand and he makes as if to kill his wife, who begs him to do it out of guilt and remorse. She claims she changed her mind about giving up her shadow. His brothers attempt to stop him from harming her, although he doesn't take much prodding.

Everyone is screaming simultaneously at everyone else as the earth suddenly opens and swallows the whole crew, except the Nurse and the Empress, in a tremendous orchestral cataclysm. The Nurse shouts that higher powers are in play. A boat appears out of nowhere. The Empress and the Nurse get in the boat and are whisked away as offstage brass fanfares, tam-tam crashes, and general mayhem bring the act to a thrilling and completely insane conclusion that invariably leaves the audience breathless and cheering. Seriously, what's not to love?

Act 3 begins with Barak and his wife in separate dark grottos. Both feel guilty and sorrowful, if for their individual reasons. A voice tells both that they may leave their cells, and they go off in search of each other. Meanwhile, the Nurse and the Empress arrive at Keikobad's, well, whatever it is—lair, den, palace, or hangout. It's very mysterious, and so is the music. The Empress claims that she is ready to face her father, but the Nurse says that death awaits her: horrible, awful, painful, excruciating, monstrous, pitiless death. "No problem," says the Empress, more or less. "See ya!" and off she goes to meet her fate.

Barak's wife and then Barak himself enter looking for each other. She wants Barak to kill her, and he just wants to give her a hug. The Nurse spitefully sends each off in the wrong direction. Then Keikobad's messenger and the Nurse have a huge argument in a really terrific scene that ends with her shrieking like a madwoman, as she gets condemned to live forever in the mortal realm. She falls devastated into the boat, which hauls her away and out of the opera entirely.

As the orchestra calms down to a lyrical violin solo, the Empress enters Keikobad's chamber. A fountain containing the "water of life," which actually kills you (it's not entirely clear what the deal is with that), springs up and a voice tells her to drink and claim Mrs. Barak's shadow. The Empress refuses and proclaims herself ready to suffer whatever judgment her father has in store for her. Over a creepy, throbbing organ pedal, with rhythmic tuned gongs and a huge crescendo followed by a roll on four offstage tam-tams, the Empress is horrified to see the Emperor already turned to stone. Only his eyes remain alive. Trust me, it's very, very cool.

The next bit is what is known in classical compositions as "melodrama": spoken text over orchestral accompaniment. Strauss clearly wanted events to move as quickly as possible, at the natural tempo of (highly emotional) speech. The Empress basically says that she is guilty enough as it is and will not make matters worse by stealing another's shadow, even if it means that her husband must suffer for her indiscretions. The voices of Barak and his wife can be heard calling to each other from offstage, while others urge her to drink, claim the shadow, and save the Emperor before it is too late. "I will NOT!" she cries, and at that moment everything falls silent. Then the high violins, like a ray of light, signal that her ordeal is over. Keikobad had been testing her.

The Emperor quickly depetrifies and joins the Empress, who now has her own unique shadow. Barak finds his wife, who also has her shadow back. The plot is over and so, in typical Straussian fashion, the singing now begins. The two couples come front and center for a truly luminous quartet intermingled with the happy voices of unborn children. Excuse me, I forgot about them; they have been driving Barak's wife crazy since act 1, lamenting her decision not to allow them to be born, but now they finally will have the opportunity, so they get to sing about that for a while too. The ensemble goes on for several minutes before bringing the opera to its joyful and satisfying close.

Really, *Frau* offers about as much sheer fun as anyone has a right to have in an operatic setting. Whether the composer and librettist meant it that way is another discussion. If you think about it seriously for more than two seconds it can all seem hopelessly silly, but while you are listening, the music creates a mesmerizing, utterly convincing universe all its own. It goes straight to the heart, bypassing the rational mind entirely, as does any fine fairy tale. And while there are serious undercurrents to this ultimately moving tale of two marriages, especially in Barak's feelings for his wife and the Empress' act 3 observations to the Nurse about the human condition, I am not going to suck all of the joy out of the work by turning sententious. Strauss lavished enough orchestral and melodic invention on this piece for ten operas. Indeed, a bad performance can very well seem to last as long as ten operas, but *Frau* is so complicated and expensive to stage or record that it's highly unlikely that you will not see and hear a very committed, thoroughly rehearsed production by singers who specialize in their roles. It's just a knockout.

In the mid-1940s, Strauss returned to *Frau* in order to fashion a Symphonic Fantasy for concert performance. It is one of his worst such arrangements, containing all of the dullest music from act 1 before petering out quietly, and it gives little hint of the opera's range or instrumental splendor. There is anecdotal evidence that Strauss did not think highly of it either. Why he did it that way is anyone's guess, but some years later conductor Erich Leinsdorf assembled a far more effective suite, which has been recorded a couple of times. If you want to sample the opera in brief, without voices, that is the version to get.

Domestic Comedies
Feuersnot, Intermezzo, and Die schweigsame Frau

Feuersnot (Fire Shortage) (1901)

Major Characters: Kunrad, the magician (baritone); the Bailiff (tenor); the Mayor (bass); Diemut, the Mayor's daughter (soprano); Elsbeth, Diemut's friend (mezzo-soprano); Wigelis, Diemut's friend (alto); Margret, Diemut's friend (soprano)

Scoring: piccolo, 3 flutes, 3 oboes, 2 English horns, 3 clarinets, bass clarinet, 3 bassoons, contrabassoon, 4 horns, 3 trumpets, 3 trombones, tuba, glockenspiel, triangle, tambourine, castanets, tam-tam, snare drum, bass drum, cymbals, 2 harps, 12 first and 12 second violins, 8 violas, 8 cellos, 6 double basses

Stage band: harmonium, 3 harps, glockenspiel, 2 snare drums, solo violin, solo cello

Feuersnot is Strauss' first revenge opera, his opportunity to give Munich the musical finger over the failure of his first opera, *Guntram*. Taking place on midsummer's eve, the townsfolk are out celebrating around a bonfire. Kunrad, a sorcerer in training and disciple of the master Reichhart Wagner (get the hint?), who was run out of town previously for his unconventional views, is in love with the mayor's daughter Diemut. She loves him too, or so it seems, but propriety forbids her from admitting their love to the stuffy citizens. So when he embarrasses her by grabbing a kiss in public, she attempts to exact revenge by hauling him halfway up to her room in a basket and leaving him there to be publicly humiliated.

Kunrad, furious, curses the town by putting out all of the fires. Appearing on Diemut's balcony, he sings a long monologue in which he castigates the citizens for their conservatism and for treating him just as badly as they treated his mentor Reichhart. The fires will remain quenched, he claims, until a virgin gives herself to him. Terrified, the townspeople beg Diemut to consummate Kunrad's passion, which she feels pretty much inclined to do anyway. Strauss' musical sex scene is unashamedly graphic and a classic example of a genre in which Strauss had no peer. It foreshadows the similar sex music introducing act 3 of *Arabella*. At its pictorial climax, the fires shoot up again to general celebration.

Musically, the piece is mature Strauss. It was his Op. 50, composed in 1901, after most of the tone poems and just before *Salome* and the *Symphonia Domestica*. The work's humor is obviously an acquired taste, and the politically incorrect handling of the relationship between Kunrad and Diemut seems to have ensured that productions would be few and far between. The opera's brevity, about ninety minutes, is also an issue, especially when you consider that it calls for fourteen solo roles plus an extensive—really extensive—part for children's choir. Operagoers generally hate children's choirs, and for good reason. They always hang around too long, and nothing they sing has anything to do with the plot.

And then there's the name, which is apt to sound like Fire-Snot in English. It's actually a compound word: *Feuers-Not*, which in its native language is pronounced more like "Foyers-Note." *Not* in German means "need," in the sense of a lack of something, but it can also mean "emergency." So "Fire Shortage" might work, but the possessive construction, "Fire's Need," also suggests Kunrad's unquenched passion, and it's used both ways in the text, which is tough enough to understand given that it employs Bavarian dialect. The librettist, Ernst von Wolzogen, was one of the founders of German cabaret and something of a character himself. He based his "sung poem," as it's subtitled, on the short story "The Extinguished Fire of Audenaerde," which is even less politically correct than the operatic version. In the original story, the woman in question is paraded naked before the town and the fire bursts forth from her rear end. Even Strauss, on the verge of *Salome*, wasn't going to touch that one.

The libretto is full of amusing wordplay, and the music is equally witty. When Kunrad describes how the town banished his predecessor, the driver (i.e., Wagner), the orchestra plays the "Valhalla" motive from *Das Rheingold*, so we know exactly whom he's thinking about. Then he claims that he, as *Der Wagner*'s successor, is ready to do battle on behalf of modern aesthetic values. *Strauss* in today's German can either mean "ostrich" or "bunch," and more colloquially "bouquet," as in a bouquet of flowers. In old German, however, since it had to mean something before the discovery of ostriches, it meant "battle." These and other inside jokes are likely to pass right over the heads of most listeners, even German ones (I tried it), and happily it makes little difference one way or the other.

Strauss' defense of Wagner against the citizens of Munich raises more than a few issues of interest. First of all, Wagner's patron, mad King Ludwig II, permitted his guest nearly to bankrupt the country. Wagner was a greedy, uncaring, egomaniacal one-man black hole when it came to money. The opposition to him was at least as much personal as it was musical. Wagner was also cohabitating with Hans von Bülow's wife, Cosima. Bülow nonetheless found himself in the excruciatingly embarrassing position of conducting the premieres of several Wagner operas, including *Tristan und Isolde*, while the composer and Cosima carried on their affair in plain view. It is not surprising that much of the citizenry, and not necessarily out of prudery but rather basic decency, took Bülow's side.

Second, one of Wagner's main antagonists on purely musical grounds was Strauss' own father, the principal horn in the Court Opera Orchestra. Franz Strauss was very much alive at the time that *Feuersnot* was composed (he died in 1905). He expressed a grumpy disapproval at the general direction of his son's compositional career, while admiring his admitted successes, and it is interesting to consider the work as the son issuing a not-too-subtle rebuke to his father. Finally, even while purporting to defend Wagner musically, the work is very much a parody of Wagnerian philosophy, especially the doctrine of "redemption through love," which Strauss replaces with "redemption through sex." Diemut's three girlfriends constitute a sort of bourgeois answer to

Wagner's three Rhine Maidens in *The Ring*, and there are other parallels as well. To that extent, the work also might be seen as a rueful critique of Strauss' own, very Wagnerian *Guntram*, despite the fact that he took its failure in Munich very hard.

On the whole, it is not difficult to explain the fact that *Feuersnot* has never really caught on with the wider public. It has been recorded a few times, quite well for the most part, but productions are still very infrequent. The work's lack of a true love interest counts against it, but then all three of Strauss' early one-act operas, including *Salome* and *Elektra*, avoid conventional love scenes with their attendant duets. More significantly, the work's smart-alecky attitude and elitist, hectoring tone can be off-putting. Nevertheless, *Feuersnot* still stands as a critical work in Strauss' output, a happy experiment if you will, and its unconventional qualities may well recommend it to many listeners leery of operatic conventions more generally. Mahler, who certainly enjoyed its subversive humor, thought it was a masterpiece, and if it remains a connoisseur's work for hardcore Strauss aficionados, there's little doubt that the composer would have understood the reasons why.

Intermezzo (1924)

Major Characters: Christine Storch (soprano); Robert Storch, her husband (baritone); Franzl, their little son (speaking role); Anna, their maid (soprano); Baron Lummer (tenor)

Scoring: piccolo, 2 flutes, 2 oboes, English horn, 2 clarinets, bass clarinet, 2 bassoons, 3 horns, 2 trumpets, 2 trombones, bass drum, cymbals, snare drum, triangle, sleigh bells, timpani, harp, piano, harmonium, 11 first violins, 9 second violins, 5 violas, 5 cellos, 3 basses

Strauss' second revenge opera is *Intermezzo*, subtitled "a bourgeois comedy with symphonic interludes," and here the object of his vengeance is also the object of his affection: his wife, Pauline. It seems that at one point she intercepted a letter from an unknown lady sent to Strauss accidentally, requesting a rendezvous. In a fury, Pauline in turn fired off a letter to Strauss demanding a divorce and even consulted an attorney. In the end it all got straightened out, but Strauss never forgot the episode, and it may be that his pride was more than a little wounded, as he was the most faithful of husbands and never did anything to suggest otherwise. Strauss wanted desperately to use this incident as the basis for a new kind of comedy, one about real life—in fact, a "reality show" in all but name. Nothing, after all, attracted Strauss more as a subject for musical characterization than his own autobiography. He tried to interest Hofmannsthal in this story, to no avail, and so he wrote the excellent libretto himself.

Now I must digress for a word or two about Hofmannsthal. Most critics and commentators regard the Strauss–Hofmannsthal partnership as one of the greatest in opera, and so it was. The audible results speak for themselves. But whatever the literary quality of the librettos that Hofmannsthal provided, and I am not in a position to judge them, I generally prefer those written by Strauss' other collaborators, merely on account of their greater clarity and directness. As a non-native speaker with a decent working knowledge of German, I only know what the librettos say, not how beautifully or intricately they say it. Besides, the success or failure of an opera never has depended on the literary value of its text independently of all other considerations.

In working with Hofmannsthal, Strauss undoubtedly felt that he was getting a good deal: a book that employed the German language with real artistry, and a major literary figure as his collaborator. This was smart from a publicity standpoint too. But he was more than a little intimidated by Hofmannsthal's erudition, and so perhaps too willing to let the writer have his way. Strauss may also have felt that he needed Hofmannsthal's ability to add philosophical depth to subjects that risked being viewed (and often were viewed) as trivial, even if today we find this straining after depth annoying, if not outright confusing.

In any event, there is just no other explanation for the existence of such conceits as the Giant Omniscient Talking Clam in *Helena*, something that Strauss would hardly have tolerated from anyone else. Hofmannsthal, to his credit, however, had no problem declining to work on subjects uncongenial to him, of which *Intermezzo* certainly was one. There was no way he could make a philosophical Big Deal out of that scenario. Given the story's complete lack of pretension—or any special need for it—he had more confidence in Strauss as his own

librettist than Strauss himself did. He was among the first to congratu-
late the composer on his achievement.

Strauss had the good sense to keep the subject of *Intermezzo* a secret
from Pauline until the premiere. How he did that was something of a
mystery, but that's how the story goes. When she found out about it,
she was furious, and the work's popular success could only have made
her angrier. Once the music's topicality wore off, however, the opera
gradually disappeared from German stages. The most ironic aspect of
the whole story is that the opera with the most personally Straussian
subject has one of the least typically Straussian scores. *Intermezzo* does
break new ground in its handling of text and music, so much so that
Strauss wrote a lengthy preface to the score (Verlag Dr. Richard Strauss,
1996; tr. Stewart Spencer), similar to that preceding *Capriccio*, to
explain what he was trying to do:

> It was in the first act of *Ariadne*, with its interplay of pure prose,
> *secco* recitative and emotionally charged recitative, that I success-
> fully essayed the vocal style that has now been taken to its logical
> conclusion in *Intermezzo*. In none of my other works, however,
> is the dialogue of greater importance than it is in this bourgeois
> comedy, which offers so few opportunities for a proper cantilena
> to develop. The symphonic element has been so carefully and
> repeatedly reworked and polished that it is often merely hinted at
> and is unable, even when the dynamic markings are imprecisely
> observed, to prevent the natural conversational tone, culled and
> copied from everyday life, from being not only heard but perfectly
> understood both in its overall context and in terms of individual
> words. It is generally only in the longer orchestral interludes that
> the lyrical element and the account of the character's psychologi-
> cal lives are more fully developed. Only in the closing scenes of
> the first and second acts is the singer given a chance to indulge in
> an extended cantilena.

Intermezzo, then, consists of a series of short scenes arranged in two
acts, with substantial orchestral interludes between them. These scenes
may include lightly accompanied *secco* recitative, more impassioned
recitative or *arioso*, spoken dialogue, and, occasionally, a genuine lyrical

outpouring. There are in fact more of these that Strauss suggests. Both the letter scene in act 1 and the card scene in act 2 contain important moments of extended song, most tellingly when the composer's wife, Christine, is thinking of her husband, and when he in turn is speaking of her to his friends while playing cards.

The actual plot concerns the aforementioned episode in the life of a conductor, Robert Storch, and his wife, Christine. She is the main character, appearing in the majority of the scenes. As the opera opens, he is leaving for an extended conducting tour, and she is feeling neglected on account of his frequent absences. While he is away, she meets a handsome young baron whom she takes under her wing for a bit of fun and harmless flirtation, until it transpires that he is looking for a "sugar momma" and asks her for money. Then she drops him like a rock. The Pauline Strauss "assignation letter" incident is repeated here with Christine, creating a similar crisis that sets up the action in act 2.

In act 2, Storch learns of his wife's decision to leave him and is thunderstruck (literally—he expresses his outrage during a thunderstorm). As the situation gets worked out, he arrives back home, where he and his wife are reconciled, and she sings without a trace of irony of their idyllic life together. Between each scene, the orchestral interludes, each of varying length, carry the emotional weight that the swiftly paced action merely suggests. The entire work plays for about two and a half hours but seems to whizz by much more quickly than that. Even the scoring is unusual: this is the only Strauss opera that asks for an odd number of strings in all sections, making the customary division of parts by desks of two players each impossible. It's a very curious indication that Strauss held this work out as something quite special, as indeed it must have been for him. Revenge, this time at least, was sweet.

Strauss arranged for concert performance a very successful suite of four movements containing five interludes from the opera. It has been recorded several times and makes an excellent independent work, particularly for those who don't have the time to listen to the complete opera, text in hand (which really is necessary). There is also an excellent live recording of the Glyndebourne Festival production of the piece in English on the Chandos label, featuring the stellar Swedish Strauss soprano Elisabeth Söderström. So the opera, which meant so much to Strauss, has been well served in a variety of formats, leaving listeners little reason not to sample it.

Die schweigsame Frau (The Silent Woman) (1935)

Major Characters: Sir Morosus, a retired admiral (bass); Henry Morosus, his nephew (tenor); Aminta, Henry's wife (coloratura soprano); Sir Morosus' housekeeper (alto); Sir Morosus' barber (baritone)

Scoring: piccolo, 3 flutes, 2 oboes, English horn, 3 clarinets, bass clarinet, 3 bassoons, contrabassoon, 4 horns, 3 trumpets, 3 trombones, tuba, glockenspiel, xylophone, small bells, large bells, snare drum, bass drum, cymbals, tam-tam, triangle, tambourine, rattle, castanets, timpani, celesta, harp, 14 first violins, 12 second violins, 8 violas, 8 cellos, 5–6 basses

Stage band: trumpets, organ, harpsichord, bagpipes, drums

Strauss' last domestic comedy ought to have been his most successful. Stefan Zweig's adaptation of Elizabethan playwright Ben Jonson's play *The Silent Woman* is genuinely funny and ideal for an operatic setting, as Strauss himself claimed. The story is similar to that of Donizetti's *Don Pasquale*: a cranky but wealthy old codger wants to marry what he thinks is a sweet, timid young girl, but she turns out to be a loud, rude shrew with an unfortunate habit for heavy spending. He can't wait to get rid of her, at which point he learns that he's been set up so that she can marry her true love.

Zweig's version had some twists guaranteed to delight Strauss. The Grumpy Old Man, Sir Morosus, can't stand noise of any kind and particularly hates music. His nephew Henry appears at the door, much to Morosus' relief, as he had vanished from school. Henry is married to Aminta and explains to his uncle that he left the university to join an opera troupe that has accompanied him to England, where the action is set. Morosus is furious and immediately disinherits his nephew and insults the members of his troupe. Morosus tells his friend, the barber, to find him a wife immediately, as he no longer has any family with which to share his time and his wealth. The barber, for his part, knows that Morosus doesn't really want to lose the love of his nephew and devises a plot to set things right.

Now comes the *Don Pasquale* maneuver. The three ladies of the opera troupe show up in disguise at the barber's behest to win the heart of Morosus. Aminta appears as "Timidia," a shy and silent woman, and naturally Morosus chooses her. Other members of the troupe arrange the sham marriage. Not only does Timidia behave in a manner that is anything but silent, she turns out to be a coloratura soprano and promptly moves a harpsichord into the house and starts taking voice lessons (from Henry in disguise). Morosus demands a divorce, and other members of the troupe appear to annul the fake marriage with a fake divorce, which turns out to be impossible because of a legal technicality. Just as Morosus finds himself on the verge of being driven crazy, Henry and Aminta reveal themselves and explain the ruse. Morosus, initially furious, has to confess that the troupe performed an excellent charade, even if he was its victim. He welcomes Henry and Aminta into his life and relaxes with happiness at the return of some much-longed-for peace and quiet.

The plot doesn't come close to suggesting the witty dialogue that carries the action along. Unlike *Intermezzo*, Strauss has a pair of young lovers woven into the storyline, so he has an excuse for integrating far more lyrical cantilena into his now patented brand of comic patter. The presence of the opera troupe also provides a welcome opportunity both for varied ensemble writing, which often has an almost Rossinian madcap verve (the finale of act 1), and a healthy fund of quotations of everything from Monteverdi's *The Coronation of Poppea* to Verdi's *Rigoletto* and Wagner's *Das Rheingold*. This lack of concern for period integrity is delicious. Strauss even wrote a full-scale comic overture (CD Track 6), which he called a "Potpourri" since it quotes the music to come. The horn theme at the start will appear as the motive symbolizing Morosus' marriage contract.

Die schweigsame Frau should have been a great success, but its run was canceled because Strauss refused to permit the Dresden authorities to omit Stefan Zweig's name as librettist. Zweig was Jewish and had fled Germany, robbing Strauss of his most promising collaborator since the death of Hofmannsthal. Strauss wrote Zweig a letter trying to persuade him, unsuccessfully as it transpired, to continue their relationship and expressing his contempt of the Nazi regime. The letter was intercepted by the Gestapo and led effectively to the final falling-out between Strauss and Hitler's government. Zweig's own story had a tragic end. Although safely out of Germany, he committed suicide in 1942.

Zweig's participation and Strauss' loyalty to him meant that *Die schweigsame Frau* was effectively banned until the end of World War II. Afterward, late Strauss was effectively banned for other reasons. He was so out of fashion musically that no one was willing to go to bat for a comedy written during the Nazi period. The logistics of opera are such that a new work has a relatively brief opportunity to establish itself in the repertoire. Sometimes an initial failure can be reversed, or success may come slowly, but *Die schweigsame Frau* was neither a success nor a failure. What is arguably Strauss' best pure comedy simply vanished.

One additional interesting fact about these three domestic comedies can be found just by looking at their scoring. Although the size and composition of the orchestra varies for each of them, you will note that Strauss asks for fewer than the usual number of basses (normally eight) in the string section. In other words, he is clearly trying to create a lighter overall sonority than we find in the tragedies and lyric dramas. Strauss himself noted that one of the differences between his writing and Wagner's is that his basic orchestral sonority is significantly higher in pitch, making it more difficult for the singers to make the text clear over the brilliance of the instrumentation. The scoring of these works, then, is very carefully calculated to permit the text to cut through the accompaniments as clearly as possible.

Although these three comedies rank among Strauss' most neglected works, the later two definitely deserve to be listed with his most effective and innovative examples of the form. Even Schoenberg liked *Intermezzo*, and he and Strauss couldn't stand each other. Part of the reason for the music's neglect stems from the fact that they are comedies in the first place. Humor is always underrated, and today's opera companies largely survive on performances of serious or tragic romantic works, with a comedy or two thrown in. Strauss, though, was first and foremost a composer of comic operas, the first of his kind since Mozart, and the only such writer of his period who did not channel his talents into lighter, exclusively comic genres, such as operetta. He wrote big, complex, musically sophisticated comedies for serious opera audiences, a task whose difficulty is easy to underestimate.

Despite his desire to be the next Offenbach, Strauss hated modern operetta as exemplified by the works of Franz Léhar (of *Merry Widow* fame). Indeed, he tried to use his position in Hitler's government to have performances restricted. It was one of his most craven and shameful acts, and he later admitted that he had been wrong to suggest it. He was jealous, of course, as well as frustrated and angry at the fact that operettas were funny and popular while his bigger, richer, and more elaborate comedies may have been funny (in varying degrees), but they were not popular. It was too much to ask that a composer who staked out his reputation on *Salome* and *Elektra* should retain the same degree of professional respect with *Die schweigsame Frau* and not be accused of slumming. In *Der Rosenkavalier* the public granted him his single comic success, just as they had Wagner and Verdi with *Die Meistersinger* and *Falstaff*, respectively. The difference is that those composers each wrote a single mature comic opera, whereas Strauss wrote at least eight.

War and Peace
Friedenstag and *Guntram*

Friedenstag (Day of Peace) (1938)

Major Characters: The Commandant (baritone); Maria, his wife (soprano); a Messenger from Piedmont (tenor); various soldiers and officers

Scoring: piccolo, 3 flutes, 2 oboes, English horn, 3 clarinets, bass clarinet, 3 bassoons, contrabassoon, 6 horns, 4 trumpets, 4 trombones, tuba, bass drum, snare drum, large tenor drum, tam-tam, timpani, 16 first and 16 second violins, 12 violas, 10 cellos, 8 basses

Stage band: organ, military trumpet, bells

Quite a few Strauss operas, as I have noted, can be said to stand among his least popular or least known, but these two really *are* his least popular and least known. Interestingly, they are related by the theme of "protest against war and violence," and you might think that this would earn them a bit of indulgence on moral grounds alone. After all, it took some courage to write a "peace opera" in 1938 Germany, particularly coming from a composer on the outs with a particularly monstrous regime. The scenario for that opera, *Friedenstag*, was moreover by the Jewish Stefan Zweig, even if Joseph Gregor wrote the actual libretto.

Okay, who are we kidding? This is opera. *Salome* is what sells. *Friedenstag*, which at seventy to seventy-five minutes plays for about the same time as many performances of Beethoven's Ninth Symphony, is hardly an opera at all. It's really more of a cantata, since the action is entirely static and it gives a major amount of singing to the chorus. It would work very well in concert and doesn't really need to be staged to have the desired effect. As an opera, it belongs to the "can belto" school, in which the story merely serves as an excuse to let everyone stand around and yell at the audience. This may be a bit of an oversimplification, but it isn't much of one.

And just look at the scoring: a Strauss opera without a harp? Indeed, a Strauss *anything* without a harp? We all know what that means: no love music, no sex music, and therefore, some would say, no Strauss music. You could argue that he deserves credit for creating an orchestral sonority uniquely suited to the subject matter, and that's a fair thought, but if the result turns out to be unappealing, he may—as the saying aptly goes in this context—have won the battle only to lose the war. In any case, it won't take you much more than an hour to find out either way. *Friedenstag* is also the only Strauss opera that takes up a single compact disc, so it's a bargain as well.

The action, such as it is, takes place at the citadel of a besieged town on the last day of the Thirty Years' War: October 24, 1648. The Thirty Years' War was a horrible mess in which religious (Catholic vs. Protestant), political (Austrians vs. French), and economic (peasants vs. everybody) crises all played a major part. In *Friedenstag*, an unnamed Catholic town stands on the verge of starvation and defeat. The populace begs the Commander of the citadel to surrender, but the Emperor has sent him a letter saying that he must hold out at all costs. Without ammunition this will prove difficult, so he decides to use the remaining gunpowder to blow up the citadel, and himself. His wife, Maria, the only named character in the opera, sings to him of her disgust at the constant warfare but decides to die with him nonetheless.

Just as the Commander lights the fuse, he hears bells in the distance. Believing the enemy to have surrendered, he extinguishes the fuse and sees the hostile forces carrying white flags, being welcomed by a joyful populace. The enemy Commander reports that a treaty has been signed and the war is over. He offers his hand to the citadel's Commander, who draws his sword. Maria throws herself between the two men and rebukes her husband for his hostility. He pauses, taking in her words, and finally embraces the enemy Commander. The people rejoice and the works ends with a jubilant choral finale.

The music, for all of this, has always seemed to me quite effective, even if it is very different from Strauss' usual modus operandi. Strauss, so the theory goes, was very much a "waltz guy" and not a "march guy," but the march music he writes in *Friedenstag* is actually pretty convincing, and the central conflict between the populace of the town and the military garrison is powerfully conveyed. Maria's scene with her husband is also telling, despite the fact that it contains little in the way of lyrical love music, no harp, and nothing at all sexual. Some have claimed that the joyful finale lacks thematic distinction, but Strauss' concern seems to have been more with the scenario's lack of theatrical viability than with his competence to set the text. In this respect, as I have already noted, he was right.

Friedenstag was originally planned as the conclusion of a double bill starting with *Daphne*. That concept didn't last very long, and it is very difficult to imagine this story following straight on Strauss' "bucolic tragedy." That left this short work out in the cold, with no theatrical partner to place it in context and give it the extra meaning originally intended. I won't say that it's impossible to imagine another work partnering with it, or that the right staging can't bring it to life. There are several fine one-act operas from the same period that might be considered: Korngold's *Violanta* and Zemlinsky's *A Florentine Tragedy* both come to mind. And let's not forget, when the Metropolitan Opera finally starting programming *Salome* three decades after its 1907 premiere, at one point it played alongside Puccini's comedy *Gianni Schicchi*. If that can be done, then anything is possible.

Guntram (1894)

Major Characters: Guntram (tenor); the old Duke (bass); Freihild, his daughter (soprano); Duke Robert, her husband (baritone); Friedhold (bass)

Scoring: piccolo, 3 flutes, 3 oboes, English horn, 3 clarinets, bass clarinet, 3 bassoons, contrabassoon, 4 horns, 3 trumpets, bass trumpet, 3 trombones, tuba, tambourine, triangle, cymbals, bass drum, tenor drum, timpani (2 players), lute, 2 harps, 16 first and 16 second violins, 12 violas, 10 cellos, 8 basses

Stage band: 4 horns, 4 tenor horns, 4 trumpets, 3 trombones, 4 snare drums

We now come to the final theatrical work up for consideration, which was also Strauss' first original opera. When a composer says of his own libretto, as Strauss did of his text for *Guntram*, "It's no worse than [Verdi's famously silly] *Il trovatore*," then you know he's grasping at straws. What makes Strauss' comment all the more telling is that it could have been even worse. Strauss spent at least five years working on the libretto of *Guntram*, far more time than he took to write the music in 1892–93. That is not a good sign. However, the work, for all its faults, represents a milestone in his development as a composer for a number of reasons, so it pays to consider it in some detail.

Act 1: In thirteenth-century Germany, Guntram and his mentor Friedhold are members of a secret society, the Champions of Love. They are knights who promote peace and love and harmony through song. They are passing out food to the starving peasant subjects of the mean and nasty Duke Robert, who has just defeated their latest rebellion. Robert's wife, the confusingly named Freihild, supports the cause of the peasants but has been forbidden to assist them further. In despair, she attempts to drown herself in the nearby lake, but Guntram rescues her, and they immediately fall in love.

Freihild's father, the old duke, who seems to have no issue with his daughter being married to an evil villain who drives her to the point of suicide, thanks Guntram and grants his request that the rebellious peasants be given their freedom. Robert, naturally, is furious. Guntram also resolves to persuade Robert through song to give up his evil ways, and they all head back to the castle to celebrate the newly declared peace. Oh yes, there's a court jester or fool who keeps interrupting and who starts most of his comments with the line "Hei-di-del-dum-dei." So far, *Il trovatore* is looking pretty good.

Act 2: At the castle, everyone is celebrating the victory of Robert over the peasants. Evidently they forgot the part about peace. Guntram is concerned at his ability to move this bloodthirsty crowd, but he and Freihild have been doing a lot of heavy-duty glancing at each other, and her expression gives him the courage to sing the "Tale of Peace." Suddenly, a messenger arrives and cries that the rebellion has broken out yet again. Robert tells his vassals to prepare for renewed war. Guntram accuses Robert of instigating the uprising and tells the vassals that he should be seized as a tyrant. Robert, true to form, tyrannically accuses Guntram of treason and attacks him, sword in hand. Guntram whips out his own sword and promptly skewers Robert, who drops dead. The old duke tells the vassals to stick Guntram in the dungeon, while Freihild, in the most Straussian moment of the whole opera, sings rapturously of the possibility of marrying Guntram once she gets him out of jail. The score is now *Il trovatore* 2, *Guntram* 0.

Act 3: In his cell, Guntram can hear priests chanting the Requiem Mass over the body of Robert. This brief moment is the first and last Christian religious episode in any Strauss opera. Freihild shows up and sings ecstatically that Guntram is now free and the two of them can get married and live happily ever after. Suddenly, Friedhold shows up—in the dungeon, which seems to have an "open door" policy—and tells Guntram in the following brilliant bit of dialogue that the Champions of Love Criminal Court is ready to judge him:

"For what?" Guntram asks.

"For your crime," Friedhold replies.

"What crime?" Guntram asks.

"Do I need to tell you?" Friedhold responds.

"Oh, *that* crime," Guntram says dismissively. "That was self-defense."

"Not exactly," Friedhold claims, explaining that even though Robert attacked him first, Guntram killed the duke knowing in his heart that he loved Freihild, and therefore he must leave her and accept punishment. Guntram, horrified, proudly states that he does not need some rinky-dink society of knights to tell him he must atone for his crime and spend the rest of his life in solitude and misery. He is perfectly capable of deciding his own degree of culpability. And so he turns to Freihild and tells her to buck up, as she's the Duchess now and the poor peasants need her. Guntram, having thus adjudicated himself guilty of loving her when he killed Robert, then leaves her—nobly, of course—to spend the rest of his life in solitude and misery.

Next to this farrago of nonsense, *Il trovatore* reads like Shakespeare, mixed-up babies and all. The difference between Strauss and your typical Italian opera libretto is that Strauss, and Wagner's school generally, had grand philosophical pretensions that the Italians couldn't have cared less about. The Germans aimed higher and consequently failed more dismally. *Il trovatore*, ridiculous plot and all, is vocally glorious and unflaggingly entertaining. "Entertaining" is not exactly a word that comes readily to mind in considering the relentlessly earnest *Guntram*, or much post-Wagnerian German opera generally, although in his very next effort, Strauss got the message. Ironically, it was the end of that third act that caused Strauss' rift with the Wagnerians, and specifically with his own real-life Friedhold, the arch-Wagnerian Alexander Ritter, who had a fit when he saw what Strauss planned to do.

You see, Ritter insisted that Guntram had to be judged by the Champions of Love, accept their punishment, and renounce Freihild. Strauss had other ideas. He composed most of the opera while convalescing in Egypt, accompanied by some light reading: Nietzsche. His exposure to the writings of Wagner's arch–ideological enemy diverted Guntram's philosophical march from the straight and narrow Wagnerian path, but only to a certain degree. Had he truly absorbed and implemented Nietzsche's thought, Strauss probably would have had Guntram tell Friedhold and the Champions of Love to go jump in Freihild's lake, then he would have settled down with her and lived happily ever after. That, however, would have been just too incongruous. So Strauss makes Guntram's self-judgment arrive at the same penalty that the Champions of Love would have imposed anyway.

It may be stupid. Guntram is saying, in effect, "I don't need you people to mess up my life when I am perfectly capable of doing it myself," but it is also the most human, realistic moment in the entire opera, since it involves a defiant exercise of free will. The characters in these post-Wagnerian essays are not people; they are symbols, or archetypes, and for that reason their actions are completely predetermined and rigidly bound to express the work's ideological program. The opera itself is not a human drama but a philosophical tract—a sermon or a morality play. In realizing that this sort of thing wasn't for him, Strauss allowed his own personal view of opera to be born. It is absolutely wonderful that we can put our finger on the exact moment that it happened with such certainty.

Guntram's significance for Strauss did not end with his dawning realization of what he wanted his operas to express. His soon-to-be wife Pauline created the character of Freihild, her only role in any of his works. Given the difficulty of his writing for the soprano voice, she may have realized that she should quit sooner rather than later. The title part is also so difficult that few tenors would willingly attempt it—just one more nail in the coffin in Strauss' relationship with that particular voice type. Around 1940, Strauss came back to *Guntram* and trimmed it down by about half an hour, thinning out the orchestration so as to make the words clearer (not necessarily a plus in this case), and bringing the running time down to just under two hours.

That said, the work easily can sound twice as long, especially as compared to later Strauss. It's a question of pacing. *Guntram* begins with a prelude clearly assembled from bits of Wagner's *Lohengrin* and *Parsifal*. It goes absolutely nowhere and takes an unconscionable twelve minutes to do it. The music itself is often very beautiful, but the progress of the action remains consistently slow. Still, there are numerous moments that foreshadow the Strauss to come, especially in the writing for Freihild and in the final duet with Guntram in act 3. Both the sententious Friedhold and the goofy jester, though, are post-Wagnerian irritants, and the overt references to Strauss' predecessor dilute the work's more original passages.

Had the music consistently sounded like top-drawer Strauss, the silliness of the story hardly would have mattered, at least to posterity; but it isn't his best effort, and the reason is because, in his heart, he didn't really have faith in his own libretto, revisions to the third act notwithstanding. The opera is patchy. His defensiveness about it speaks volumes, as does the fact that he felt the necessity to lick his wounds for eight years before writing an entire "revenge opera" to make his point. One of the ironies about his next opera, *Feuersnot*, is that while it mocks the people of Munich for their conservatism, *Guntram* really is in fact a conservative, or at least derivative, work.

Indeed, the opera was cautiously successful at its premiere in Weimar in 1894, and both the audience and the critics in Munich in 1895, at the work's single staging, evidently were at least respectful. Strauss' recollection of a fiasco seems to have been selective and was likely linked to the turmoil associated with the production (the orchestra went on strike to protest the music's difficulty; some of the singers rebelled too—the usual operatic insanity). The public in any case never had a chance to get to know the piece, because the additional performances that Strauss had been promised never materialized. *Guntram* was just dropped from the repertoire.

Strauss was used to getting his way as a composer and generally enjoyed provoking his listeners and causing a scandal, but *Guntram* was different. This time, perhaps for the first time, it was personal, and he fully expected a straightforward success. He had pushed all the right Wagnerian buttons, and the one deviation from ideological orthodoxy was hardly going to be noticed by nonbelievers, nor was it the reason for the work's failure. The opera disappointed, for the most part, on purely musical grounds, as Strauss tacitly admitted in making those revisions in his final decade. It was a lesson that he never forgot. Whether his future efforts succeeded or failed, it would be very much on his own terms, as Strauss and no one else.

Over Forty Gorgeous Songs with Orchestra (Who Knew?)

trauss composed about two hundred songs for voice and piano, and he orchestrated forty-one of them. Other composers arranged even more, including the most popular individual song, "Zueignung" ("Dedication"—CD Track 7). Indeed, Strauss' own orchestration wasn't made until 1940 and is still often overlooked. This explains one reason why so many of his song arrangements remain unknown: they were made individually, either for specific singers (including his wife), or during difficult times of forced inactivity in the creation of larger works, as you will see from the dates in the list below.

Also, while Strauss published groups of songs under a single opus number, sometimes gathered together by poet, they were seldom intended as coherent cycles unified by theme, as in Mahler's *Songs of a Wayfarer* or *Kindertotenlieder*. Where Strauss did orchestrate an entire opus, as in the six *Brentano Lieder* of Op. 68 for soprano, their wildly differing orchestration, vocal requirements, and subject matter make it awkward to program them in a single concert. Even complete recordings are rare. The entire set in any case was only scored over a seven-year period, beginning with the last of them, the turbulent "Lied der Frauen" ("Song of the Women [While Their Men Are at War]"). That song requires the vocal heft of a dramatic soprano, which is a far cry from the coloratura of "Amor," the penultimate number. Some of Strauss' collections also contain songs for more than one voice type, such as soprano and baritone in Op. 56, making them impossible for the same singer to perform together. Only the last two songs in that group were orchestrated.

Or consider the two songs for low voice of Op. 44, "Notturno" and "Nächtlicher Gang" ("Nocturnal Passage"). The former is a nocturnal meditation for a selectively refined ensemble, lasting between fifteen and twenty minutes. It is Strauss' longest single song. The latter piece is a wild ghost story for massive orchestra that's over in a flash—about six minutes. You will seldom if ever hear them played together. Indeed, "Nächtlicher Gang" has been recorded only once, in the single complete collection of the orchestral songs (on Nightingale recordings).

Ironically, the one collection of Strauss songs that everyone knows and loves, the glorious *Four Last Songs*, isn't a collection at all. Granted, they work beautifully together as they stand, especially with "Im Abendrot" ("In Twilight"—CD Track 8) as the conclusion of the group with its final question, "Is this perhaps death?" and the horns' and violas' quotation of the "transfiguration" theme from the eponymous tone poem (at 6:08). Nevertheless, Strauss scholar Timothy L. Jackson has made a very persuasive case that these songs were intended to complete a cycle begun with the earlier "Ruhe, meine Seele!" ("Be Still, My Soul!"), which Strauss orchestrated at the very end of his life, at the same time as the composition of the *Four Last Songs*. The scoring alone seems to bear this out.

On the other hand, there is simply no excuse why the *Three Hymns*, Op. 71, aren't equally as popular as the *Four Last Songs*; they come from the same sound world and partake of a similarly captivating lyric impulse. The second of them, "Rückkehr in die Heimat" ("Return Home"), with its swirling arpeggios for harp and celesta, is one of the most magical settings that Strauss ever made. Both performances and recordings, however, remain disappointingly few and far between. It may be that the sentimental historical context of the *Four Last Songs* has made it unthinkable that Strauss could have written something just as fine in 1921.

Strauss' "art songs" are the most artistic of a genre that was destined, at least originally, for domestic performance. In other words, like all of his music, they demand professional singers with well-trained voices. They make few if any concessions to the amateur market. Indeed, even a simple love song in three verses like "Zueignung," with its refrain of "Habe Dank!" ("Be thankful!"), approaches the melody from a strange harmonic angle guaranteed to throw off anyone but a seasoned artist, and Strauss varies each verse subtly. The music is thus more interesting, but also more difficult.

Many of the songs sound like fragments taken straight from the operas, especially love songs like the rapturous "Cäcilie," the serene "Morgen!" ("Tomorrow!"), or the erotically charged and voluptuous "Verführung" ("Seduction"). "Die heiligen drei Könige aus Morgenland" ("The Three Holy Kings from the Orient") offers one of the few examples of a Strauss setting a text on a religious theme, although one gets the impression that the descriptive opportunities of the words are what really attracted him. Elsewhere, we find songs on some familiar Straussian themes: "Gesang der Apollopriesterin" ("Song of the Priestess of Apollo") could have come from one of the Greek operas; "Meinem Kinde" ("My Child") was composed for Pauline during her pregnancy, and he followed it up with the lovely "Wiegenlied" ("Lullaby").

Strauss' habit of ending a melody with a particularly difficult phrase or in a vocally awkward position—check out "Winterliebe" ("Winter Love")—indicates that his wife must have been technically quite gifted, since he claimed that no one sang his songs better. He composed over a hundred of them between 1885 and 1906, many with her voice in mind (they met in 1887), and he orchestrated several for her use in their concerts together. After she retired from concertizing around 1906, his song output slowed considerably, except for certain special occasions inspired by particular singers, and orchestrations of music written much earlier.

So if you don't have time for a complete opera, the songs offer a very useful and rewarding alternative, especially since you don't have to deal with any of Strauss' repeated experiments with the relationship between text and musical setting in recitative. The songs contain pure Straussian lyricism of the kind that most voice fans value above all. Moreover, they are every bit as comprehensive in their range and variety as any of his works in larger media.

The following contains a roughly chronological list of all of Strauss' songs for voice and orchestra, including dates of composition or publication and orchestration (where different). The scoring of each song is also given, because as usual it says so much about the infinite variety of colors and textures that Strauss obtains, often from strikingly limited resources. I also hope that singers or members of community and chamber orchestras might review this list and realize that there is actually quite a bit of top-notch Strauss that does not require outsize forces and that deserves to be played and enjoyed by musicians and audiences alike.

Find a couple of enterprising young singers looking for exposure (no shortage of those), and add a little imagination, and some really beautiful programs of familiar and lesser-known *Lieder* could be assembled quite easily. And remember, these are only the songs that Strauss orchestrated himself; there are at least five additional arrangements made by others that he personally approved.

"Zueignung" ("Dedication") (1907, orch. 1940)
Scoring: 2 flutes, 2 oboes, 2 clarinets, 3 bassoons, 4 horns, 3 trumpets, 2 harps, timpani, strings

"Ruhe, meine Seele!" ("Be Still, My Soul!") (1894, orch. 1948)
Scoring: piccolo, 2 flutes, 2 oboes, English horn, 2 clarinets, bass clarinet, 2 bassoons, 4 horns, 2 trumpets, 3 trombones, tuba, harp, celesta, timpani, strings

"Cäcilie" (1894)
Scoring: 2 flutes, 2 oboes, 2 clarinets, 2 bassoons, 4 horns, 2 trumpets, 3 trombones, tuba, harp, timpani, strings

"Morgen!" ("Tomorrow!") (1894)
Scoring: 3 horns, harp, solo violin, strings

"Liebeshymnus" ("Hymn of Love") (1896)
Scoring: 3 flutes, 2 oboes, 2 clarinets, 2 bassoons, 4 horns, trumpet, 4 solo violins, strings

"Verführung" ("Seduction") (1897)
Scoring: 3 flutes, 2 oboes, English horn, 2 clarinets, bass clarinet, 3 bassoons, 4 horns, 2 harps, timpani, strings

"Gesang der Apollopriesterin" ("Song of the Priestess of Apollo") (1896)
Scoring: 3 flutes, 3 oboes, 3 clarinets, 3 bassoons, contrabassoon, 4 horns, 3 trumpets, 4 trombones, cymbals, timpani, strings

"Hymnus" (1897)
Scoring: 2 flutes, 2 oboes, 2 clarinets, bass clarinet, 2 bassoons, 4 horns, 2 trumpets, 3 trombones, harp, triangle, timpani, strings

"Pilgers Morgenlied" ("Pilgrim's Morning Song") (1897)
Scoring: piccolo, 2 flutes, 2 oboes, 3 clarinets, 3 bassoons, 4 horns, 2 trumpets, 3 trombones, tuba, timpani, strings

"Das Rosenband" ("The Rose Ribbon") (1898)
Scoring: piccolo, 2 flutes, 2 oboes, 2 clarinets, bass clarinet, 2 bassoons, 2 horns, strings

"Ich liebe dich" ("I Love You") (1898, orch. 1943)
Scoring: 2 flutes, 2 oboes, 2 clarinets, 2 bassoons, 4 horns, 2 trumpets, 3 trombones, timpani, strings

"Meinem Kinde" ("My Child") (1898)
Scoring: 2 flutes, 2 bassoons, harp, solo strings

"Mein Auge" ("My Eye") (1898, orch. 1933)
Scoring: 2 flutes, 2 oboes, 2 clarinets, 2 bassoons, 2 horns, trumpet, harp, strings

"Befreit" ("Freed") (1898, orch. 1933)
Scoring: 2 flutes, 2 oboes, English horn, 2 clarinets, bass clarinet, 2 bassoons, contrabassoon, 4 horns, 2 trumpets, 3 trombones, tuba, harp, harmonium, timpani, strings

"Wiegenlied" ("Lullaby") (1916)
Scoring: 2 flutes, 2 oboes, English horn, 2 clarinets, 2 bassoons, 3 horns, 2 harps, 3 solo violins, 2 solo violas, strings

"Muttertändelei" ("Mother-talk") (1900)
Scoring: 2 flutes, 2 oboes, English horn, 2 clarinets, 2 bassoons, 2 horns, triangle, cymbals, strings (without basses)

"Notturno," Op. 44, No. 1 (1899)
Scoring: piccolo, 2 flutes, 2 oboes, English horn, 2 clarinets, bass clarinet, 2 bassoons, contrabassoon, 3 trombones, strings

"Nächtlicher Gang" ("Nocturnal Passage"), Op. 44, No. 2 (1899)
Scoring: 2 piccolos, 4 flutes, 2 oboes, English horn, 3 clarinets, 2 bassoons, contrabassoon, 6 horns, 4 trumpets, 3 trombones, tuba, harp, bass drum, cymbals, tam-tam, castanets, rute (stick bundle), xylophone, timpani, strings

"Des Dichters Abendgang" ("The Poet's Evening Walk") (1900, orch. 1918)
Scoring: 3 flutes, 2 oboes, English horn, 2 clarinets, bass clarinet, 2 bassoons, 4 horns, 3 trumpets, 3 trombones, tuba, 2 harps, timpani, strings

"Freundliche Vision" ("Friendly Vision") (1901, orch. 1918)
Scoring: 2 flutes, 2 bassoons, 4 horns, 2 trumpets, 2 trombones, strings

"Winterweihe" ("Winter Consecration") (1901, orch. 1918)
Scoring: oboe, 2 clarinets, 2 bassoons, 3 horns, strings

"Winterliebe" ("Winter Love") (1901, orch. 1918)
Scoring: piccolo, 2 flutes, 2 oboes, 2 clarinets, 2 bassoons, 4 horns, 2 trumpets, 3 trombones, snare drum, cymbals, timpani, strings

"Waldseligkeit" ("Forest Bliss") (1902, orch. 1918)
Scoring: 2 flutes, 2 clarinets, bass clarinet, 2 bassoons, 2 horns, harmonium, harp, strings (12, 12, 8, 8, 6)

"Das Thal" ("The Valley"), Op. 51, No. 1 (1902)
Scoring: 3 flutes, 2 oboes, 2 clarinets, 2 basset horns, bass clarinet, 2 bassoons, contrabassoon, 4 horns, 2 trumpets, strings (12, 12, 8, 8, 6)

"Der Einsame" ("The Lonely One"), Op. 51, No. 2 (1906)

Scoring: 3 flutes, 2 clarinets, 2 basset horns, bass clarinet, 2 bassoons, contra-bassoon, strings (12, 12, 8, 8, 8)

"Frühlingsfeier" ("Spring Celebration"), Op. 56, No. 5 (1906, orch. 1933)

Scoring: piccolo, 2 flutes, 2 oboes, English horn, 2 clarinets, bass clarinet, 2 bassoons, contrabassoon, 4 horns, 2 trumpets, 3 trombones, harp, cymbals, timpani, strings

"Die heiligen drei Könige aus Morgenland" ("The Three Holy Kings from the Orient"), Op. 56, No. 6 (1906)

Scoring: 3 flutes, 2 oboes, English horn, 2 clarinets, 3 horns, 2 trumpets, 3 trombones, tuba, triangle, tambourine, bass drum, cymbals, timpani, 2 harps, celesta, strings

"An die Nacht" ("To the Night"), Op. 68, No. 1 (1919, orch. 1940)

Scoring: 2 flutes, 2 oboes, English horn, 2 clarinets, bass clarinet, 2 bassoons, 4 horns, 3 trumpets, 3 trombones, harp, timpani, strings

"Ich wollt ein Sträusslein binden" ("I Would Have Made a Bouquet"), Op. 68, No. 2 (1919, orch. 1940)

Scoring: 2 flutes, 2 oboes, 2 clarinets, 2 bassoons, 2 horns, harp, strings

"Säusle, liebe Myrthe" ("Whisper, Dear Myrtle"), Op. 68, No. 3 (1919, orch. 1940)

Scoring: 2 flutes, 2 oboes, 2 clarinets, 2 bassoons, 2 horns, strings

"Als mir dein Lied erklang" ("Your Song Rang Out to Me"), Op. 68, No. 4 (1919, orch. 1940)

Scoring: 2 flutes, 2 oboes, 2 clarinets, bass clarinet, 2 bassoons, 2 horns, 2 trumpets, harp, strings

"Amor," Op. 68, No. 5 (1919, orch. 1940)

Scoring: flute, oboe, clarinet, bass clarinet, bassoon, strings (no basses)

"Lied der Frauen" ("Song of the Women [While Their Men Are at War]"), Op. 68, No. 6 (1919, orch. 1933)

Scoring: piccolo, 2 flutes, 2 oboes, English horn, 2 clarinets, bass clarinet, 2 bassoons, contrabassoon, 4 horns, 2 trumpets, 3 trombones, tuba, 2 harps, bass drum, tam-tam, timpani, strings

Three Hymns, Op. 71 (1921)

No. 1: "Hymne an die Liebe" ("Hymn to Love")

No. 2: "Rückkehr in die Heimat" ("Return Home")

No. 3: "Die Liebe" ("Love")

Scoring: piccolo, 3 flutes, 2 oboes, English horn, 3 clarinets, bass clarinet, 3 bassoons, 4 horns, 3 trumpets, 3 trombones, tuba, 2 harps, celesta, timpani, strings

"Das Bächlein" ("The Little Brook") (1935) [famously, and depressingly, dedicated to Joseph Goebbels]

Scoring: 2 flutes, 2 oboes, 2 clarinets, bass clarinet, 2 bassoons, 2 horns, harp, strings

Four Last Songs (1948)

No. 1: "Im Abendrot" ("In Twilight")

No. 2: "Frühling" ("Spring")

No. 3: "Beim Schlafengehn" ("Going to Sleep")

No. 4: "September"

Note: The above order is as published in the complete edition of the songs. The normal performing order is 2, 4, 3, 1.

Scoring: 2 piccolos, 2 flutes, 2 oboes, English horn, 2 clarinets, bass clarinet, 3 bassoons, contrabassoon, 4 horns, 3 trumpets, 3 trombones, tuba, harp, celesta, timpani, strings

Conclusion

There are an extraordinary number of valid ways to look at Strauss' output: as a love affair with the human voice, as an exploration of everything that the modern orchestra can do, as the end of a great musical tradition, as the start of a new one, or as an effort to find new relationships between words and music. Strauss worked in all of these areas, and with a remarkable degree of success. And that's not all. As I write these words, I am looking at a nine-disc set of chamber music: piano trios, the string quartet, cello sonata, violin sonata, piano sonata, a disc of music for horn and piano, a string trio, and the melodramas for voice and piano, among other pieces. Most of it is early, and not all of it is good, but much of it is. Not distinctive, perhaps, or essential, but good.

Strauss positively dripped music. It is astonishing that he was able to retain the focus necessary to create as much as he did, for as long as he did, given the situation in Germany during the latter half of his life. Because his career stretched on for nearly seventy years, it tells a sobering story. As long as his own personal development coincided with the path that German music was taking, he was its most famous and successful representative. There was a period when Strauss truly *was* German music. They were synonymous. Not even Wagner achieved that, because Brahms stood in the way, but after 1895 there was no one but Strauss for at least the next two decades. Nevertheless, when music went left and Strauss went right, he became irrelevant. It's really that simple.

However, this only describes the historical side of things. It says nothing about the quality of his music considered as music. Strauss continued to write masterpieces after World War I because, forgetting all that first-rate, second-rate composer nonsense, he was a great and gifted musician. He followed an individual path, true to himself, even as he never quite grasped that German music was bigger than he was in the same way that he understood that it was bigger than Wagner. Was he then a hypocrite, or just an artist with all that this implies? It seems that the answer is clear.

Appendix
Starting a Strauss Collection

All of Strauss' most popular works have been recorded countless times, and extremely well, while some of his less famous pieces can still be difficult to find. None of the music described in this book lacks for adequate recordings, except perhaps the First Symphony. The current state of the record industry at the time of writing makes it very difficult to say what will be in print at any point, or even on which labels the best performances may appear. Recordings and artists formerly associated with a single label can turn up as budget releases licensed to another, while the availability of digital downloads makes the very notion of specific "labels" offering proprietary product a nebulous concept.

Keeping this in mind, one way to start building a collection is to follow the lead of the great Strauss conductors. Herbert von Karajan recorded most of the tone poems multiple times, as well as superb renderings of *Der Rosenkavalier* (his first EMI recording, with Elisabeth Schwarzkopf as the Marschallin, now part of Warner Classics), *Salome*, and *Ariadne auf Naxos*. Karajan's Vienna Philharmonic version of *Also sprach Zarathustra* for Decca was the performance used in the film *2001: A Space Odyssey*, but his subsequent remake with the Berlin Philharmonic on Deutsche Grammophon is much better, as are his Berlin recordings of the tone poems more generally.

There are two other sets of Strauss orchestral music that permit you to get a big chunk of his best-known output in a convenient, exceptional, and inexpensive boxed set. The first of these contains Fritz Reiner's Chicago recordings on RCA (now Sony/BMG), while the second is a nine-disc set featuring all of the tone poems, the concertos, and many other suites and shorter works in astoundingly fine performances by Rudolf Kempe leading Strauss' favorite orchestra, the Staatskapelle Dresden, on EMI (Warner Classics). This is the go-to set and the bedrock of any serious Strauss collection, and samples can be found on the CD that comes with this book. Kempe also made an outstanding recording of *Ariadne*.

All of Strauss' operas have been recorded at least once, but not all of them come with librettos, an aggravating trend that you will have to work around if you want to know what the vocalists are singing about. One option is to purchase videos wherever these are available, since they almost invariably feature subtitles in multiple languages, and opera, as a theatrical medium, is meant to be seen as well as heard. An amazing crop of DVDs has been released in recent years, including rarities such as *Arabella*, *Intermezzo*, *Die Frau ohne Schatten*, *Josephs Legende*, and *Capriccio* alongside the expected trove of *Salome*s, *Elektra*s, and *Rosenkavalier*s. The only problem with DVDs is that, while often very good, they seldom contain the best performances or sonics. One exception is Catherine Malfitano's *Salome*, conducted by the late Giuseppe Sinopoli, an amazing and horrifying (in a good way) performance not to be confused with her Covent Garden video under Dohnányi, which is less gripping.

Guntram boasts but a single recording, fortunately reissued at budget price by Sony, while *Feuersnot* has been recorded several times, but an English translation of the text is all but impossible to find. Georg Solti presided over an excellent series of Strauss operas for Decca, mostly made in Vienna, including *Salome*, *Elektra*, *Der Rosenkavalier*, *Ariadne auf Naxos*, and the reference recordings of *Arabella* and *Die Frau ohne Schatten*. The *Salome* and *Elektra* feature legendary soprano Birgit Nilsson, the *Arabella* Lisa Della Casa. Karl Böhm's versions of *Elektra*, *Daphne* (he was the opera's dedicatee), and *Capriccio* on Deutsche Grammophon are especially noteworthy, as are Wolfgang Sawallisch's performances of Strauss' last opera, plus rarities such as *Friedenstag* and *Intermezzo* (all for EMI/Warner).

There is only a single set of Strauss' complete songs with orchestra, on the Nightingale label with a fine assortment of singers. British soprano Felicity Lott has recorded an extensive selection of them, beautifully sung, for the Chandos label, which also has a very impressive Strauss catalogue featuring Neeme Järvi and the Scottish National Orchestra. This includes many vocal and orchestral rarities (such as the Violin Concerto and Second Symphony). Elisabeth Schwarzkopf's song recital with conductor George Szell on EMI/Warner is also a classic, while Strauss fans retain a special affection for the disc containing the *Four Last Songs* and other *Lieder* sung with unparalleled richness of tone at excruciatingly slow tempos by soprano Jessye Norman, with Kurt Masur leading the Leipzig Gewandhaus Orchestra (Philips).

Those recordings offer just a sample of the Strauss discography but are more than sufficient to get started on a very serious collection. There is no logic to what the record industry does. At the present time, it is easy to find the complete wind serenades (featuring the outstanding Netherlands Wind Ensemble on Newton Classics) but very difficult to source the Couperin Dance Suites and *Schlagobers*. All of that may change in short order. In any case there is no need to rush, and with a composer as rich and diverse as Strauss, there is always the promise of a new discovery.

CD Track Listing

1. *Don Juan*

   Rudolf Kempe, conductor, Staatskapelle Dresden
   From EMI CD 6 78312 2 CD2

2. *Daphne*: Transformation Scene

   Kiri Te Kanawa (Daphne); Julius Rudel, conductor, Philharmonia
   Orchestra
   From EMI CD 5 56417 2

3. *Der Rosenkavalier*: "Ist ein Traum"

   Natalie Dessay (Sophie), Angelika Kirchschlager (Octavian);
   Antonio Pappano, conductor, Orchestra of the Royal Opera House,
   Covent Garden
   From Virgin Classics CD 6 41933 2

4. *Salome*: "Dance of the Seven Veils"

   Rudolf Kempe, conductor, Staatskapelle Dresden
   From EMI CD 6 78312 2 CD1

5. *Salome*: Closing Scene

   Nina Stemme (Salome); Antonio Pappano, conductor, Orchestra of the
   Royal Opera House, Covent Garden
   From EMI CD 3 78797 2

6. *Die schweigsame Frau*: Potpourri

   Jeffrey Tate, conductor, Rotterdam Philharmonic Orchestra
   From EMI CD 7 54581 2

7. "Zueignung"

    Elisabeth Schwarzkopf, soprano; George Szell, conductor, Berlin Radio
    Symphony Orchestra
    From EMI CD 0 87318 2

8. "Im Abendrot" (from *Four Last Songs*)

    Elisabeth Schwarzkopf, soprano; George Szell, conductor, Berlin Radio
    Symphony Orchestra
    From EMI CD 0 87318 2